RMT Exam Guide

A Walk Through the Blue Print

The Association for Healthcare Documentation Integrity

Rebecca McSwain, PhD, CMT

Publisher: Association for Healthcare Documentation Integrity
Author: Rebecca McSwain, PhD, CMT
Managing Editor: Lea M. Sims, CMT, AHDI-F
Copyeditor: Kristin Wall, CMT, AHDI-F
Professional Programs Manager: Kelly Kappmeier
Interior Design: Lea M. Sims, CMT, AHDI-F
Cover Design: Network Media Partners, Inc.

AHDI
4230 Kiernan Avenue, Suite 130
Modesto, CA 95356
800-982-2182
www.ahdionline.org

DISCLAIMER

ISBN 978-0-93522960-8

Printed in the United States of America

To purchase additional copies of this book, call our member services department at (800) 982-2182 or purchase this text online at www.ahdionline.org.

Look for AHDI on Facebook, Twitter, and Linked In under *Association for Healthcare Documentation Integrity*. Visit our blog at http://www.ahdilounge.org/.

"Excellence is a better teacher than mediocrity. The lessons of the ordinary are everywhere. Truly profound and original insights are to be found only in studying the exemplary."

– Warren G. Bennis

Table of Contents

Acknowledgements

On behalf of AHDI, I would like to extend our gratitude to the following association leaders and experts who assisted in the preparation of this workbook through blue print item-writing. As always, we are appreciative of the passion these individuals have for preparing our next generation workforce for professional credentialing:

Kirk Calabrese, MA, CMT
Christette Cromarty, RMT
Tanya Guenther, CMT, AHDI-F
Donna Lockey, CMT
Jackie Stockton, CMT
Constance Walls, CMT

In addition, we would like to acknowledge the hard work and contributions of our Professional Programs staff, outstanding team players who made sure we met our deadlines for this manuscript:

- *Kristin Wall, CMT, AHDI-F,* for providing her professional expertise and vigilant copyediting and serving as an invaluable resource on this project.
- *Kelly Kappmeier* for applying her project management training and organizational skills to execute this text on a fast-track schedule.
- *Tina Wilson* for much-needed support and coordination as well as excellent oversight of other departmental priorities while our professional staff focused on this manuscript.

Thank you to the 2010 House of Delegates, who acknowledged the important goal of legitimizing transcription/editing as a risk management and regulatory compliance profession by passing a resolution in August 2010 that called for the mandatory credentialing of all professionals who have access to protected health information through the documentation process.

Finally, to the author of this text—*Rebecca McSwain, PhD, CMT*—thank you for putting your expertise and eloquence to the page. AHDI and the industry we serve are very blessed to have you on staff. You have brought a wealth of experience and scholarly wisdom to our Professional Programs Department. It is a *great* pleasure to work with you.

Lea M. Sims, CMT, AHDI-F
Director of Professional Programs, AHDI

How to Use This Book

This text is designed to be used as a supplemental study guide in preparation for the AHDI Registered Medical Transcriptionist (RMT) exam. Students and practitioners who seek access to the RMT exam need to begin that process of preparation with a strong orientation to the exam blue print.

This book provides potential exam candidates with a "walk through the blue print," the goal of which is to make sure that the RMT candidate has a clear understanding of the industry's expectations of competency for a Level 1 candidate and the content domains against which a candidate will be evaluated on the exam. This *RMT Exam Guide: A Walk Through the Blue Print* is, by design, an orientation specifically to the cognitive assessment (multiple-choice) objectives housed on the blue print.[1]

Each chapter contains a *Chapter Overview* to orient the reader to exam objectives and competencies being addressed in the chapter as well as a bulleted list of what skills related to those objectives are critical to the execution of the MT/editor skill set at Level 1. Beyond that, each chapter offers the following organizational approach to intentional, focused study for each RMT objective covered in the chapter:

- *Statement of Objective* from the RMT Blue Print

- *Rationale* that explains the importance of that exam objective and why its inclusion on the exam blue print is important for demonstrating level 1 competency as an RMT

- *Recommendations for Focused Study,* with a list of recommended texts and corresponding chapters and sections to aid in directed study against the blue print objective

- *Sample Questions* that demonstrate the scope and format of potential exam questions and give the candidate a feel for the type of questions that may be asked under that blue print objective

---

[1] The audio objectives on the RMT Blue Print are **not** addressed here but will be addressed in the audio volume of this text to be published/released by summer of 2011.

Once a candidate has worked his/her way through this guide, the text will offer a *Practice Test*, a 97-question test designed to simulate the weight and balance of cognitive assessment (multiple-choice) items found on the RMT exam and allow the candidate to diagnose areas of weakness and assess needs for further study.

Housed in the appendices of this text is a full copy of the RMT blue print (*See: Appendix B: RMT Blue Print Check List*) formatted to allow candidates to check off each blue print objective when it has been studied and mastered. The appendices also contain other valuable resources related to AHDI credentialing exams and assessment aids and products.

If you have any questions or need further assistance related to this text, please feel free to forward your inquiries to credentialing@ahdionline.org.

Foreword

Congratulations for embarking on the path to achieving the Registered Medical Transcriptionist (RMT) credential from the Association for Healthcare Documentation Integrity (AHDI). Whether you are just starting the journey or well on your way to a successful professional career in health information management, AHDI certification in medical transcription with a Level 1 credential (RMT) or Level 2 certification via the Certified Medical Transcriptionist (CMT) is your guide to career enhancement, increased recognition, and greater success in your profession.

AHDI credentials are earned through a challenging program of examinations, education, and experience, and maintained through continuous review and education. Earning an AHDI credential puts you in a special category, positioning you as a role model for others in the field of healthcare documentation. Investing in AHDI certification is an investment in yourself and your long-term career that opens the door to more opportunities for career advancement. Certification can increase your job mobility and choices even in the face of a tough job market.

Candidates who begin down the road of credentialing frequently want to know what the difference is between certification and licensure. Certification is a nongovernmental process of regulation within a community, profession, organization, occupation, or a specialty within a profession. Certification is a voluntary process based on select eligibility set forth by the organization, derived from industry standards of practice and a thorough job analysis. On the other hand, licensure may be defined as a mandatory credentialing process established by a government entity, usually at the state level. Licensure is rooted in the legal concept of the regulatory power of the state. This power holds that the state has the right and obligation to pass laws and take other necessary actions to protect the health, safety, and welfare of its citizens. Passage of a state licensure or credentialing law for a given profession restricts or prohibits the practice of that profession by individuals not meeting state-determined qualification standards, and violators may be subject to legal sanctions such as fines, loss of license to practice, or imprisonment.

Although certification is voluntary and not required to practice medical transcription, it does attest to the fact that the holder of the credential has met the standards of the credentialing organization and is therefore entitled to make the public aware of this as further documentation of his or her professional competence.

The question then becomes: *Why obtain your credential from AHDI if an individual need not be certified in order to practice as a medical transcriptionist?* Professionals in many disciplines have long debated this question. In the case of medical transcription, certification differentiates the professional competencies of medical transcriptionists from those of other allied health disciplines. This designation is especially important in today's climate of electronic delivery of health information. With new and emerging technologies to capture, display, and transmit health information, competition within the medical transcription and clinical documentation sector is increasing from technology vendors like speech recognition and electronic medical record systems.

A credentialed workforce can demonstrate the value that human intelligence can bring to the technology used to capture and deliver health information and to produce accurate, complete health records. Competency-based professional credentials inform the public and the healthcare community that there is a distinct body of knowledge and set of skills required to perform this work. Furthermore, the interpretive nature and application of informed judgment as well as the ability for medical transcriptionists to amend or modify the record makes it critical that the sector have benchmarks and standards to assess job readiness and reliability in risk management of healthcare documentation.

To be sure, healthcare professionals place a high value on licensure, credentials, and professional designations. Credentials tell others on the healthcare delivery team that medical transcriptionists are a legitimate allied health profession with an accountable scope of practice. In fact, recent privacy and security changes outlined in HIPAA regulations intended to provide greater safeguards, as the healthcare systems move toward adoption of electronic health record systems will make it important for our sector to demonstrate training and certification in HIPAA compliance. The implementation of ICD-10 coding in the United States health system will also require greater document specificity, requiring other health professionals to rely more heavily on the accuracy and completeness of records generated with the expertise of medical transcriptionists.

When taking into consideration all these changes on the horizon, it is no wonder that industry employers are moving toward preferential hiring practices for credentialed professionals, a position supported by the employer members of the

Clinical Documentation Industry Association (formerly the Medical Transcription Industry Association). Whether you are a new graduate entering the healthcare documentation sector or a practicing medical transcriptionist readying yourself to sit for the RMT exam, we hope this workbook will serve you well in your preparation as you go through the exercises in this workbook and explore the exam blue print. W Good luck with your studies and with successfully passing the exam.

Peter Preziosi, PhD, CAE
Chief Executive Officer
Association for Healthcare Documentation Integrity

Section 1

Transcription Standards and Style

"Credentialing! I am all for it, and always have been. It is like getting an education – you simply cannot get anywhere without it and the same goes for getting credentialed, be it RMT or CMT! Go for it! I did and I know my employer is proud of me for doing so and for making his life a bit easier. He knows he is in good hands and he appreciates that." – Jean J. (JJ) Zwang, CMT

The Legal Record

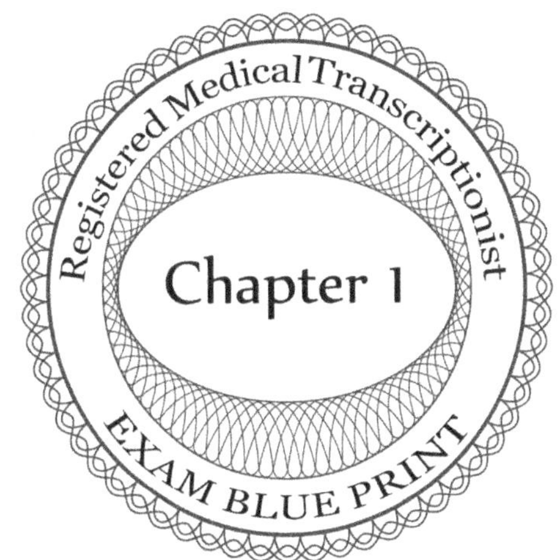

"If medical transcriptionists were only required to 'type what they hear' and apply the standards as outlined throughout this book, the role would be a relatively straightforward one. A skilled, engaged MT partners with the physician to ensure an accurate, timely, and secure record."

– The Book of Style for Medical Transcription, 3e

Chapter Overview

Information is one of the most important aspects of medicine; for example, scientific research is useless unless results are reliable and disseminated. Likewise, patient care is inadequate if accurate and timely information about the individual's current health and course of treatment is not available. As members of the healthcare documentation team, medical transcriptionists share responsibility for the accuracy and integrity of the healthcare record upon which excellent patient care depends. In addition, risk management, coding for reimbursement, and statistical analysis to achieve both individual and public health goals all depend upon a reliable flow of information from healthcare provider to coders, administrators, and scientists. Occupying a critical position in the documentation workflow, between origination by the healthcare provider and the finalized legal document that is the healthcare record, the transcriptionist performs a vital role in the creation of clinical information that meets the needs of patients, providers, and the medical community.

The body of knowledge for Level 1 medical transcriptionists therefore includes an understanding of:

- The types of healthcare documents, their standard forms, and contents.

- How clinical information is organized, presented, and tracked.
- When editing by the transcriptionist is appropriate, and strategies for situations in which editing is not appropriate.
- How to ensure precision in the language of the healthcare document.
- The legal requirements for safeguarding the security and privacy of healthcare documents.

There are **12 objectives**[1] on the RMT blue print that address concepts related to these domains and against which an RMT exam candidate will be evaluated. In this chapter, we will walk through each objective listed under *RMT Blue Print Section 1: Transcription Standards of Style* that relate to these domains.

Objectives 1.1 and 1.2

Objective 1.1: *Given sample report content or subheading, identify the report type (autopsy, consultation, correspondence, discharge summary, history and physical examination, operative report, pathology report, or SOAP note) that the information would be transcribed under.*

Objective 1.2: *Identify the correctly expressed report headings or subheadings.*

Rationale

In terms of patient care and safety, quality control and risk management, it is important for the transcriptionist to understand how the whole range of information in patient care documentation is organized: where does a specific kind of information belong, and what is the relationship of that content to other levels or types of information? This knowledge will become increasingly important as electronic record-keeping is more widely adopted, and the organization of clinical information becomes more standardized. The medical transcriptionist, for example, will be able to recognize whether a healthcare provider has used the correct template for accurate patient-care documentation: a hurried physician may

---

[1] Objective 1.6 on the RMT blue print is an audio objective that also relates to the Legal Record. Look for blue print guidance on audio objectives in upcoming AHDI exam prep products.

inadvertently choose an inappropriate report template from a drop-down menu. Further, a medical transcriptionist who is knowledgeable about the components of various report types will be able to assist in the creation of report templates, using her/his knowledge of the appropriate content for various report types.

Recommendations for Focused Study

1. *The Book of Style for Medical Transcription, 3rd Edition*
   Chapters 1, 25, and 26
2. *The Book of Style 3rd Edition Workbook*
   Chapter 1
3. *AHDI Exam Prep Flash Cards: Healthcare Record & Medicolegal Issues*

Sample Questions

Each question below represents the kind of format and content, per the exam blue print, that an RMT candidate can expect to find on the RMT exam. *Note: These are sample questions only. They are questions that do not currently appear on the RMT exam. Though some may represent items retired from previous exam forms, not all items have been psychometrically analyzed, and AHDI cautions candidates against the presumption that these items alone may be diagnostic or indicative of candidate performance.* **(Answer key at end of chapter.)**

1. **The area was prepared and draped in the usual sterile manner.**

   In which type of report would the above excerpt be transcribed?

   A. Progress note
   B. Discharge summary
   C. History and physical
   D. Operative report

2. In which report would the phrase "*cranial nerves are intact*" likely be documented?

   A. Autopsy
   B. Operative report
   C. Pathology report
   D. History and physical examination

3. **There is marked tenderness over McBurney point.**

Under what physical examination subheading would this observation be transcribed?

A. HEENT
B. Chest
C. Abdomen
D. Neurologic

4. **Specimens sent for frozen section reveal a desmoplastic stromal response.**

Under which report heading would this statement be found?

A. PHYSICAL EXAMINATION
B. INVESTIGATIONS
C. DIAGNOSIS
D. MICROSCOPIC DESCRIPTION

Objective 1.3

Objective 1.3: *Identify the role/purpose of time and date stamping in transcription.*

Rationale

It is vitally important both for patient care and for legal protection of healthcare providers that the integrity of the healthcare record be safeguarded. For those reasons, continuity and timing of record creation is protected by noting the date and time of creation on each record. The transcriptionist must understand the importance of date and time stamping in maintaining the integrity of the healthcare document.

Recommendations for Focused Study

The Book of Style for Medical Transcription, 3rd edition; Section 1.2.9.

Sample Questions

Each question below represents the kind of format and content, per the exam blue print, that an RMT candidate can expect to find on the RMT exam. *Note: These are sample questions only. They are questions that do not currently appear on the RMT exam. Though some may represent items retired from previous exam forms, not all items have been psychometrically analyzed, and AHDI cautions candidates against the presumption that these items alone may be diagnostic or indicative of candidate performance.* (**Answer key at end of chapter.)**

5. What is the purpose of date and time stamping in medical transcription?

   A. To allow reimbursement
   B. To help create an audit trail
   C. To indicate the date treatment was provided
   D. To identify the transcriptionist

6. Which expression is included in the record to meet HIPAA security requirements?

   A. AXIS II
   B. T1NXMX
   C. T: 12/31/11, 1500
   D. *Dictated by not read.*

Objectives 1.4, 1.5, and 1.7

Objective 1.4: *Given dictated sentences, identify the one that would require editing on the part of the transcriptionist.*

Objective 1.5: *Given dictated sentences, identify the one that contains an incorrectly used term or one that contains transposed terms or values. Identify the slang terms or back formations.*

Objective 1.7: *Given a scenario of encountering a contextual inconsistency or irreconcilable word or phrase, identify the proper procedure for correction and/or notification.*

Rationale

The medical transcriptionist works with the healthcare provider to create an accurate and reliable document. To achieve this goal, transcriptionists have always acted as editors of the finished healthcare document. With the coming of the electronic health record and with increasing use of speech recognition and other automated systems to create drafts of documents, that editorial function is becoming more and more critical. The medical transcription practitioner must recognize when editing is necessary, which requires an understanding of correct grammatical structure, the ability to detect misuses of medical terminology, and the knowledge of what kinds of slang terms or back formations need editing. On the other hand, the medical transcriptionist must exercise informed judgment about when to refrain from editing, and about the procedures to be used when editing is not appropriate.

Recommendations for Focused Study

1. *The Book of Style for Medical Transcription, 3rd Edition*
   Section 2 – Chapter 28 and Appendix B
2. *The Book of Style 3rd Edition Workbook*
   Chapter 2
3. *AHDI Statement on Verbatim Transcription*
   AHDI website (www.ahdionline.org) - Advocacy

Sample Questions

Each question below represents the kind of format and content, per the exam blue print, that an RMT candidate can expect to find on the RMT exam. *Note: These are sample questions only. They are questions that do not currently appear on the RMT exam. Though some may represent items retired from previous exam forms, not all items have been psychometrically analyzed, and AHDI cautions candidates against the presumption that these items alone may be diagnostic or indicative of candidate performance.* **(Answer key at end of chapter.)**

7. Which sentence would require editing by the medical transcriptionist?

   A. Both the patient and I received the laboratory results.
   B. Both I and the patient received the laboratory results.

C. Laboratory results were forwarded to the patient and I.
D. Laboratory results were forwarded to the patient and me.

8. Which dictated sentence requires editing by the transcriptionist?

A. He complains of pain in the right shoulder, inability to sleep at night, and difficulty raising his arm.
B. He complains of having right shoulder pain, being unable to sleep at night, and having difficulty raising his arm.
C. He complains that he has pain in the right shoulder, is unable to sleep at night, and has difficulty raising his arm.
D. He complains of right shoulder pain, unable to sleep at night, and difficulty raising his arm.

9. Which sentence contains slang that requires editing by the transcriptionist?

A. I requested a crit level on this patient.
B. This physician carried out an exam on the patient.
C. Before the procedure, a sterile prep was performed.
D. The lab results showed elevated eos.

10. Which contains transposed values?

A. Hemoglobin 42, hematocrit 14.
B. WBC 8500 and RBC 5.2.
C. The pH is 5.2. Specific gravity is 1.020.
D. Normal differential showing 50% segs and 1% eos.

11. **DICTATED: The patient saw Dr. Arif Shah for a 2nd opinion.**

In the scenario above, the dictator does not spell the doctor's name. Which of the following is the best way to transcribe the sentence?

A. The patient saw another doctor for a 2nd opinion.
B. The patient saw Dr. ________ for a 2nd opinion.
C. The patient saw Dr. R. F. Shaw for a 2nd opinion.
D. The patient saw Dr. (sounds like R. F. Shaw) for a 2nd opinion.

12. The physician is dictating the results of an MRI into an office note. He is interrupted in the middle of a sentence. When he returns, he does not continue with the MRI, but begins dictating recommendations. What is the correct action to take?

   A. Stop transcribing, delete the report, send the audio file back to the main queue, and begin another job.
   B. End the MRI dictation at the last complete sentence, continue with the remainder of the report, and submit the report.
   C. End the MRI dictation in mid-sentence as dictated, continue with the remainder of the report, and submit the report.
   D. End the MRI dictation in mid-sentence as dictated, continue with the remainder of the report, and flag the report for the physician.

Objectives 1.8 – 1.12

Objective 1.8: *Given abbreviations related to health record privacy, identify the correct expanded form.*

Objective 1.9: *Identify appropriate examples of PHI and/or disclosure of PHI under the HIPAA privacy rule.*

Objective 1.10: *Identify the individuals and/or organizations that are defined as accountable parties or business associates under the HIPAA rule.*

Objective 1.11: *Identify appropriate security measures for protecting PHI.*

Objective 1.12: *Identify the recommended encryption standard of healthcare records under the HIPAA security rule.*

Rationale

Since 1996, the US Congress has enacted two major pieces of legislation related to the security and privacy of the healthcare record, HIPAA and HITECH (the latter as part of the American Recovery and Reinvestment Act of 2009). As guardians of the integrity of the healthcare documentation process, medical transcriptionists must understand the content of these laws, the rules by which they are applied to healthcare documentation, and the procedures required to remain under compliance with those rules. Medical transcriptionists working as independent contractors should be specifically mindful of the rules and regulations that apply to business associations, since business associates who provide contracted services to healthcare facilities are held accountable to all the same requirements as the healthcare facility itself.

Recommendations for Focused Study

1. *The Book of Style for Medical Transcription, 3rd Edition*
   Chapter 3
2. *The Book of Style 3rd Edition Workbook*
   Chapter 3
3. *Ethical Best Practices: Resource Guide for Healthcare Documentation Specialists*
   Section 4

Sample Questions

Each question below represents the kind of format and content, per the exam blue print, that an RMT candidate can expect to find on the RMT exam. *Note: These are sample questions only. They are questions that do not currently appear on the RMT exam. Though some may represent items retired from previous exam forms, not all items have been psychometrically analyzed, and AHDI cautions candidates against the presumption that these items alone may be diagnostic or indicative of candidate performance.* (**Answer key at end of chapter.)**

13. What does HIPAA stand for?

    A. Health Insurance Portability and Access Act
    B. Health Information Portability and Accountability Act
    C. Health Insurance Portability and Accountability Act
    D. Health Information Portability and Insurance Act.

14. Under HIPAA definition, what does PHI stand for?

    A. Protected Health Information
    B. Patient Health Information

C. Privileged Health Information
D. Private Health Information

15. According to HIPAA, PHI includes information in what form?

A. On paper
B. On paper and electronically transmitted
C. On paper, electronically transmitted, and orally transmitted
D. Electronically and orally transmitted

16. Which would be a violation of the HIPAA privacy rule?

A. Releasing information relating to patient's care to a third-party insurance billing company
B. Disclosing information about an individual's health in a phone call between physicians providing care for the same patient
C. Releasing information about a patient's health status to public health authorities
D. Using a de-identified health record for clinical study or statistical research

17. Which individual is considered an accountable party under the HIPAA rule?

A. An employee of a covered entity
B. An employee of a transcription service
C. A business associate of a covered entity
D. An employee of a federally funded healthcare facility

18. Which characteristic determines that an offshore transcription service is considered a business associate under HIPAA?

A. It employs US-based transcriptionists.
B. It contracts directly with a covered entity.
C. It subcontracts to a US-based business associate.
D. It performs transcription services involving US-based patients.

19. Which is a precaution recommended in sending PHI by fax?

A. Transmit faxes only at night, when offices are empty.
B. Transmit only de-identified health information.

C. Transmit using pre-programmed client fax numbers.
D. Transmit faxes only after notifying the recipient by phone that the fax is coming.

20. What is recommended for fax machines transmitting PHI?

A. Use them only for transmitting PHI.
B. Locate them in a secured area.
C. Use only certain models especially designed for PHI.
D. Allow only one designated individual to use them.

21. Under the HIPAA security rule, when is it recommended to encrypt health information?

A. Only when downloading information
B. Only when uploading information
C. When transmitting information over some networks
D. When transmitting information by fax

Objective 1.13

Objective 1.13: *Identify documentation authentication practices considered dangerous by both the Joint Commission and DHHS.*

Rationale

Medical transcriptionists are first and foremost data integrity managers. Data integrity refers to the *validity* of the data. MTs guard the integrity of health information through prudent physical and "cyber" protective practices, but they also partner with the provider to ensure that the *information* itself is not compromised. This means being able to understand and identify unsafe documentation authentication practices – ie, practices whereby a healthcare encounter is documented without reasonable and credible authentication by the provider.

Recommendations for Focused Study

1. *The Book of Style for Medical Transcription, 3rd Edition*
   Chapter 3

2. *The Book of Style 3rd Edition Workbook*
   Chapter 3
3. *Ethical Best Practices: Resource Guide for Healthcare Documentation Specialists*
   Section 4

Sample Questions

Each question below represents the kind of format and content, per the exam blue print, that an RMT candidate can expect to find on the RMT exam. *Note: These are sample questions only. They are questions that do not currently appear on the RMT exam. Though some may represent items retired from previous exam forms, not all items have been psychometrically analyzed, and AHDI cautions candidates against the presumption that these items alone may be diagnostic or indicative of candidate performance.* **(Answer key at end of chapter.)**

22. What authentication practice is considered dangerous by Joint Commission?

    A. Electronic signature
    B. Autosignature
    C. Handwritten signature
    D. Handwritten initials

23. What is the Joint Commission's position on authentication of the healthcare record?

    A. Any credentialed healthcare provider may appropriately authenticate any health record.
    B. Authentication cannot be delegated to anyone other than the author of the record.
    C. Authentication may be delegated to the proper ancillary medical personnel.
    D. The author of the record may assign responsibility for document accuracy to the medical transcriptionist.

Sample Questions Answer Key

1. D
2. D
3. C
4. D
5. B
6. C
7. C
8. D
9. A
10. A
11. B
12. D
13. C
14. A
15. C
16. A
17. C
18. B
19. C
20. B
21. C
22. B
23. B

English Language

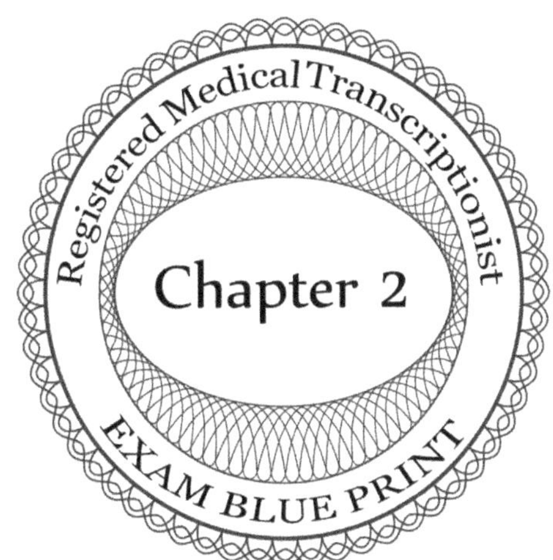

"Strong language skills are critical to the skilled MT, and they will often make the difference between an average transcriptionist and an excellent one. If the provider dictates, 'Lungs is clear,' the MT will be expected to recognize the error in grammar and correct it."

– The Book of Style for Medical Transcription, 3e

Chapter Overview

The English language, like all other known languages, has rules about how it should be used. Utterances, whether written or spoken, are structured in specific ways according to those rules. Such linguistic rules evolve over time to maintain clarity and coherence within the community of speakers of the language: unless grammatical rules (and others, such as rules about pronunciation) are followed, accurate communication becomes impossible. In medicine, in particular, accurate, clear, and coherent communication is the essential basis of excellence in clinical practice and in scientific research. The medical transcriptionist brings to the process of healthcare documentation a broad grasp of both the rules of English and how the language is used in the context of clinical practice. This skill set helps ensure the creation of accurate, clear, and coherent healthcare documents.

The body of knowledge for medical transcriptionists therefore includes an understanding of:

- Correct English grammar, with ability to recognize common usage errors.
- The appropriate usage of homonyms, heteronyms, and other words commonly confused for one another.
- The correct use of punctuation in abbreviations and value expressions.

- Correct capitalization.
- Correct expression and usage of plurals, including commonly used words from Latin.
- Correct expression of possessives.
- How to ensure precision in the language of the healthcare document.
- The legal requirements for safeguarding the security and privacy of healthcare documents.

There are **6 objectives**[1] on the RMT blue print that address concepts related to these domains and against which an RMT exam candidate will be evaluated. In this chapter, we will walk through each objective listed under *RMT Blue Print Section 1: Transcription Standards of Style* that relate to these English language domains.

Objective 1.14

Objective 1.14: *Given sentences with usage errors (subject/verb agreement, pronoun/antecedent agreement, who vs. whom), identify the one containing correct usage.*

Rationale

In transcribing or editing healthcare documents, the medical transcriptionist must be able to recognize both spoken errors of English usage (as in dictation) and written usage errors (as in those in a computer-generated document). One of the most common errors will be failure of agreement of subject and verb: a singular subject requires a singular verb, and a plural subject requires a plural verb. Often sentence structure will confuse this issue, as when the subject and verb are separated by intervening clauses, or when there is confusion about whether a subject noun is actually singular or plural in form. Another class of common errors involves pronoun usage. For example, there will often be confusion about whether the correct pronoun form is the objective or the subjective case. Far from being minor, these errors have the potential to significantly obscure meaning, and in medical

[1] Objectives 1.16 and 1.21 on the RMT blue print are audio objectives that also relates to English Language. Look for blue print guidance on audio objectives in upcoming AHDI exam prep products.

documents a patient's safety may depend upon clarity. As part of the health documentation team, the medical transcriptionist contributes knowledge of correct usage to enhance healthcare documentation clarity and accuracy.

Recommendations for Focused Study

1. *The Book of Style for Medical Transcription, 3rd Edition*
   Chapters 4 and 5
2. *The Book of Style 3rd Edition Workbook*
   Chapter 5
3. *The AMA Manual of Style, 10th Edition*
   Section 2, Chapter 7
4. *The Gregg Reference Manual, 11th Edition*
   Part 1 – Grammar, Usage, and Style (Section 11: Usage)

Sample Questions

Each question below represents the kind of format and content, per the exam blue print, that an RMT candidate can expect to find on the RMT exam. *Note: These are sample questions only. They are questions that do not currently appear on the RMT exam. Though some may represent items retired from previous exam forms, not all items have been psychometrically analyzed, and AHDI cautions candidates against the presumption that these items alone may be diagnostic or indicative of candidate performance.* **(Answer key at end of chapter.)**

1. Which sentence is grammatically correct?

   A. Neither of the patients is following the protocol.
   B. Dr. Jones, as well as the family, are making the decision.
   C. Either the physician or the nurse practitioner are monitoring the patient.
   D. Every one of the patients are responsible for participating in the program.

2. Which sentence correctly uses the pronouns?

   A. We need to determine whom is the patient's primary care provider.
   B. To me, there is no question whom is the right provider for this patient.
   C. Advise him who to send the report to.
   D. I would like to know who signed the report.

Objective 1.15

Objective 1.15: *Given sentences containing English words commonly confused for other words, identify the correct sentence.*

Rationale

One of the factors affecting clear communication in English is the fairly common occurrence of words that are confused with other words. Often the confusion is based upon the fact that the words sound alike or are spelled alike, but sometimes usage errors even involve words that are unrelated in terms of spelling or pronunciation. Even highly educated individuals can make these kinds of word choice errors, and sometimes mistaken word usage actually spreads like a virus, particularly within a given community. However, even when frequently used, these choices are still erroneous and pose a threat to the clarity and integrity of the healthcare document. The medical transcriptionist or editor will be thoroughly familiar with correct word choice and will be able to assist the healthcare provider in ensuring the integrity of patient-care documents.

Recommendations for Focused Study

1. *The Book of Style for Medical Transcription, 3rd Edition*
   Chapters 4 and 5
2. *The Book of Style 3rd Edition Workbook*
   Chapter 5
3. *The AMA Manual of Style, 10th Edition*
   Section 2, Chapter 11
4. *The Gregg Reference Manual, 11th Edition*
   Part 1 – Grammar, Usage, and Style (Section 11: Usage)

Sample Questions

Each question below represents the kind of format and content, per the exam blue print, that an RMT candidate can expect to find on the RMT exam. *Note: These are sample questions only. They are questions that do not currently appear on the RMT exam. Though some may represent items retired from previous exam forms, not all items have been psychometrically analyzed, and AHDI cautions candidates against the presumption that these items alone may be diagnostic or indicative of candidate performance.* (**Answer key at end of chapter.)**

3. Which sentence is correct?

   A. In lieu of chemotherapy, he opted for alternative therapy.
   B. Surgery is not an option, in lieu of his condition.
   C. In lieu of metastases, surgery is not an option.
   D. Surgery was performed in lieu of the emergent situation.

4. Which sentence demonstrates correct word choice?

   A. The information was discussed between her, him, and me.
   B. The information was discussed between her, I, and her husband.
   C. The information was discussed among she, I, and her husband.
   D. The information was discussed among her, her husband, and the son.

Objective 1.17

Objective 1.17: *Given sentences or phrases, select the one that represents correct use of punctuation.*

Rationale

The use of punctuation enables correct interpretation of a written language; furthermore, the pauses and other vocal modifications suggested by punctuation are an aid to understanding spoken language as well. Thus, correct punctuation is particularly important in medical communications, where accuracy and legibility are crucial to so many aspects of patient care, scientific research, and financial operations. Given that fact, the medical transcriptionist must be very knowledgeable about the rules of punctuation. However, the medical transcriptionist must also be aware that rules about punctuation are somewhat fluid, flexible, and subject to individual preferences. Keeping in mind the overall goal of absolute clarity of communication, the transcriptionist will work with basic rules (understanding how those rules may evolve) and with individual preferences, to maximize clarity. As the electronic health record becomes more widely adopted, some punctuation rules are likely to be modified; the transcriptionist, as editor, must accommodate those modifications without compromising the integrity of the record.

Recommendations for Focused Study

1. *The Book of Style for Medical Transcription, 3rd Edition*
   Chapter 6
2. *The Book of Style 3rd Edition Workbook*
   Chapter 6
3. *The AMA Manual of Style, 10th Edition*
   Section 2, Chapter 8
4. *The Gregg Reference Manual, 11th Edition*
   Part 1 – Grammar, Usage, and Style (Sections 1 & 2)

Sample Questions

Each question below represents the kind of format and content, per the exam blue print, that an RMT candidate can expect to find on the RMT exam. *Note: These are sample questions only. They are questions that do not currently appear on the RMT exam. Though some may represent items retired from previous exam forms, not all items have been psychometrically analyzed, and AHDI cautions candidates against the presumption that these items alone may be diagnostic or indicative of candidate performance.* (**Answer key at end of chapter.)**

5. Which sentence is correctly punctuated?

   A. The patient was seen, on June 12, 2010 in the office.
   B. The patient was seen on June 12, 2010, in the office.
   C. The patient was seen on June 12, 2010 in the office.
   D. The patient was seen on June 12 2010, in the office.

6. Which sentence represents correct use of punctuation marks?

   A. The FEV, FVC ratio is 80%.
   B. Office hours will be from 8-12 noon on weekdays.
   C. It was decided to re-treat the site of infection.
   D. Tumor is stage T1-NO-MO.

Objective 1.18

Objective 1.18: *Given words or sentences, identify the one that represents correct expression of capitalization.*

Rationale

Capitalization in written language serves the function of marking structural elements (eg, the beginning of a sentence) and of providing emphasis, significance, or distinction for certain words. As with other rules about language, rules governing capitalization are subject to change over time and to individual or community preferences, and debate about the use of capitalization is ongoing in the English language, as in medical communications. The medical transcriptionist must exercise judgment, based on knowledge of current usage, the nature of specific words (*When is a word a proper name versus a common noun?*), and facility preference.

Recommendations for Focused Study

1. *The Book of Style for Medical Transcription, 3rd Edition*
   Chapter 7
2. *The Book of Style 3rd Edition Workbook*
   Chapter 7
3. *The AMA Manual of Style, 10th Edition*
   Section 2, Chapter 10
4. *The Gregg Reference Manual, 11th Edition*
   Part 1 – Grammar, Usage, and Style (Section 3: Capitalization)

Sample Questions

Each question below represents the kind of format and content, per the exam blue print, that an RMT candidate can expect to find on the RMT exam. *Note: These are sample questions only. They are questions that do not currently appear on the RMT exam. Though some may represent items retired from previous exam forms, not all items have been psychometrically analyzed, and AHDI cautions candidates against the presumption that these items alone may be diagnostic or indicative of candidate performance.* (**Answer key at end of chapter.)**

7. Which of the following phrases is correctly transcribed?

A. Two individuals were involved in the accident: The patient and his mother.
B. The most important question is: How many individuals were involved?
C. The patient's history indicated 2 individuals were involved; the Patient and his mother.
D. I asked the police officer, how many individuals were involved?

8. Which sentence represents correct capitalization?

A. The patient was given Penicillin.
B. Cultures were positive for Escherichia coli.
C. The patient is a chinese female.
D. Local Anesthesia was used for the procedure.

Objective 1.19

Objective 1.19: *Given words or sentences, identify the one that reflects correct expression of a plural or given a Latin singular form, identify the correct plural form or given a Latin plural form, identify the correct singular form.*

Rationale

The medical transcriptionist, whether creating or editing a document, will need to understand the correct formation of plurals, including plural forms for Latin words commonly used in English. As with all aspects of the healthcare record, clarity of communication is the essential basis for all applications, whether it be for patient care, reimbursement, or scientific research. Given an increasing use of structured data as the electronic health record evolves, consistency in these formations will become crucial for reliable data capture and transmission. The transcriptionist must understand the rules for plural forms and be able to recognize errors in both dictated and computer-generated records. The transcriptionist must also be able to apply an educated judgment to whether the use of singular or plural forms is appropriate in various contexts.

Recommendations for Focused Study

1. *The Book of Style for Medical Transcription, 3rd Edition*
   Section 8.1
2. *The Book of Style 3rd Edition Workbook*
   Chapter 8
3. *The AMA Manual of Style, 10th Edition*
   Section 2, Chapter 9
4. *The Gregg Reference Manual, 11th Edition*
   Part 1 – Grammar, Usage, and Style (Section 6: Plurals and Possessives)

Sample Questions

Each question below represents the kind of format and content, per the exam blue print, that an RMT candidate can expect to find on the RMT exam. *Note: These are sample questions only. They are questions that do not currently appear on the RMT exam. Though some may represent items retired from previous exam forms, not all items have been psychometrically analyzed, and AHDI cautions candidates against the presumption that these items alone may be diagnostic or indicative of candidate performance.* (**Answer key at end of chapter.)**

9. Which phrase includes the correct expression of the singular form of *nares*?

   A. The patient's left nare.
   B. The patient's left naris.
   C. The patient's left nares.
   D. The patient's left narus.

10. Which is expressed correctly?

   A. HEENT: Sclerae were anicteric.
   B. The patient had severe mitral regurgitation with a bluish right sclerae.
   C. Sclera were clear bilaterally.
   D. Amyloid infiltration of both sclera had been identified.

Objective 1.20

Objective 1.20: *Given words or sentences, identify the one that reflects correct expression of a possessive.*

Rationale

In the interest of clarity and accurate communication, the correct formation of possessives is important, and this may be particularly the case with the formation of possessives for plural nouns. When a report is describing injuries, for example, in a context where there may be multiple patients involved, it is critical to distinguish whether a particular description applies to one individual or to more than one. Given a dictation such as "The victims extremities showed evidence of blunt trauma," how can the record convey whether one victim or many victims evidenced trauma? The medical transcriptionist who understands (from the context of the dictation) that more than one victim is referenced will transcribe "The victims' extremities showed evidence of blunt trauma," thus making the dictator's meaning clear. The transcriptionist knows that placement of an apostrophe can transform the meaning of an English sentence!

Recommendations for Focused Study

1. *The Book of Style for Medical Transcription, 3rd Edition*
   Section 8.2
2. *The Book of Style 3rd Edition Workbook*
   Chapter 8
3. *The AMA Manual of Style, 10th Edition*
   Section 2, Chapter 7
4. *The Gregg Reference Manual, 11th Edition*
   Part 1 – Grammar, Usage, and Style (Section 6: Plurals and Possessives)

Sample Questions

Each question below represents the kind of format and content, per the exam blue print, that an RMT candidate can expect to find on the RMT exam. *Note: These are sample questions only. They are questions that do not currently appear on the RMT exam. Though some may represent items retired from previous exam forms, not all items have been psychometrically analyzed, and AHDI cautions candidates against the presumption that these items alone may be diagnostic or indicative of candidate performance.* (**Answer key at end of chapter.)**

11. Which phrase shows a correct possessive expression concerning the whole Smith family?

    A. The Smith's house
    B. The Smiths house
    C. The Smiths' house
    D. The Smith house

12. Which sentence demonstrates correct use of a possessive?

    A. Has the population reached it's limits?
    B. Has the population reached its' limits?
    C. Has the population reached its's limits?
    D. Has the population reached its limits?

Sample Questions Answer Key

1. A
2. D
3. A
4. D
5. B
6. C
7. B
8. B
9. B
10. A
11. C
12. D

Abbreviations

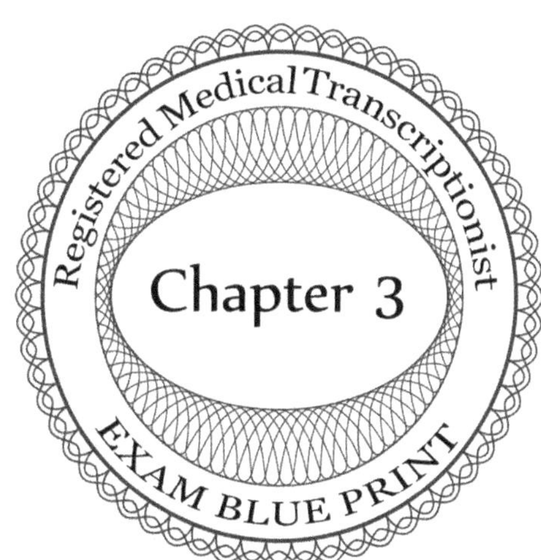

"The use of abbreviations in health encounter documentation is widely prevalent. The primary consideration for the expansion or retention of a dictated abbreviation should be the promotion of clarity. Attention must be paid to the potential for misinterpretation when encountering abbreviations in dictation."

– The Book of Style for Medical Transcription, 3e

Chapter Overview

Brief forms, abbreviations, acronyms, and initialisms are widely used in medicine and can provide a useful shorthand way to communicate longer or more complex words or ideas. However, the use of abbreviations can also compromise document clarity and integrity, and, therefore, many organizations involved in healthcare documentation (such as the American Medical Association, the Joint Commission, and AHDI) generally discourage the overuse of these short forms. Abbreviated forms that seem obvious to one healthcare provider may prove to be obscure to other readers of the document, and this can be a problem for patient care and for other applications of documentation, for example for coding and reimbursement. It is the responsibility of the medical transcriptionist to assist originators of the healthcare record in the proper use of short forms in clinical reports, in order to promote patient safety and document accuracy for any and all purposes.

The body of knowledge for medical transcriptionists therefore includes an understanding of:

- The correct meaning and use of Latin abbreviations frequently used in medicine.

- The appropriate use of abbreviations in healthcare documentation, recognizing that in some elements of the document abbreviations must never be used.
- The abbreviations identified by the Joint Commission and international standard-setting bodies as dangerous or potentially dangerous to patient care and safety.

There are **3 objectives**[1] on the RMT blue print that address concepts related to these domains and against which an RMT exam candidate will be evaluated. In this chapter, we will walk through each objective listed under *RMT Blue Print Section 1: Transcription Standards of Style* that relate to these domains.

Objective 1.22

Objective 1.22: *Given a definition, identify the correct Latin abbreviation, or given a Latin abbreviation, identify the correct definition.*

Rationale

Latin, the language of medicine for centuries, has contributed many commonly used short forms to the medical lexicon. These are among the most widely used and widely understood abbreviations in clinical documentation. The medical transcriptionist is expected to know the meanings of those abbreviated Latin terms in order to assist in monitoring the accuracy of documentation and to ensure that the document created does accurately reflect the intent of the healthcare provider and the reliable delivery of patient care. Such quality monitoring may be particularly important in the realm of medication dosages and scheduling.

Recommendations for Focused Study

1. *The Book of Style for Medical Transcription, 3rd Edition* Chapter 9
2. *The Book of Style 3rd Edition Workbook,* Chapter 9

---

[1] Objective 1.25 on the RMT blue print is an audio objective that also relates to Abbreviations. Look for blue print guidance on audio objectives in upcoming AHDI exam prep products.

3. *The AMA Manual of Style, 10th Edition*
   Section 3, Chapter 14
4. *The Gregg Reference Manual, 11th Edition*
   Part 1 – Grammar, Usage, and Style (Section 5: Abbreviations, 545)

Sample Questions

Each question below represents the kind of format and content, per the exam blue print, that an RMT candidate can expect to find on the RMT exam. *Note: These are sample questions only. They are questions that do not currently appear on the RMT exam. Though some may represent items retired from previous exam forms, not all items have been psychometrically analyzed, and AHDI cautions candidates against the presumption that these items alone may be diagnostic or indicative of candidate performance.* **(Answer key at end of chapter.)**

1. What is the correct definition for the Latin abbreviation a.c.?

   A. With food
   B. By mouth
   C. By injection
   D. Before food

2. Which of the following is the correct abbreviation for "as needed"?

   A. q.n.
   B. p.r.n.
   C. q.o.d.
   D. p.c.n.

Objective 1.23

Objective 1.23: *Given sentences containing dictated abbreviations, identify the one that requires expansion under the DIAGNOSIS or OPERATIVE TITLE headings.*

Rationale

Even though abbreviations, acronyms, and other short forms may be useful for succinctly communicating longer ideas and words, there are areas within the clinical report where absolute clarity is so important that short forms should never be used. Given their potential for misinterpretation, abbreviations need to be expanded in areas of the report where ongoing clinical and reimbursement decisions are dependent. Those areas of the report (DIAGNOSIS and OPERATIVE TITLE sections) that are used for coding a care encounter for potential reimbursement should be free of abbreviations that might interfere or hinder that process. The medical transcriptionist must be able to identify those areas of clinical reports requiring expansion of all short forms; and this obviously requires that the transcriptionist know the correct expansion of those forms!

Recommendations for Focused Study

1. *The Book of Style for Medical Transcription, 3rd Edition*
   Chapter 9: Sections 9.1.7 and 9.1.8
2. *The Book of Style 3rd Edition Workbook*
   Chapter 9

Sample Questions

Each question below represents the kind of format and content, per the exam blue print, that an RMT candidate can expect to find on the RMT exam. *Note: These are sample questions only. They are questions that do not currently appear on the RMT exam. Though some may represent items retired from previous exam forms, not all items have been psychometrically analyzed, and AHDI cautions candidates against the presumption that these items alone may be diagnostic or indicative of candidate performance.* **(Answer key at end of chapter.)**

3. Which phrase contains an abbreviation that would require expansion under the heading DIAGNOSIS?

   A. Advanced CAD.
   B. End-stage AIDS.
   C. Forearm laceration, 3 cm.
   D. Prostatic enlargement with elevated PSA.

4. Which phrase contains an expression that requires expansion when used under a DISCHARGE DIAGNOSIS heading?

A. Status post lumbar fusion of L1 through L3.
B. Status post spinal reconstruction with TLIF.
C. Status post repair of 5 cm laceration to the forearm.
D. Status post AIDS-related kidney failure.

Objective 1.24

Objective 1.24: *Identify the abbreviations found on the Joint Commission's* Do Not Use *list of dangerous abbreviations.*

Rationale

Abbreviations can be used safely and effectively in healthcare documentation. At the same time, unwise overuse of abbreviations can confuse and obscure the meaning of a document, posing threats to patient safety and to the effectiveness of patient care. The use of abbreviations has long been a contentious issue in healthcare documentation, and the role of the transcriptionist is to apply, as much as possible, accepted community standards for abbreviated terms. Various national and international bodies in the medical and scientific communities have set standards for abbreviations; the standards of most relevance for medical transcription are set by the Joint Commission and the US Department of Health and Human Services. The medical transcription practitioner must have a thorough knowledge of these standards, and in particular must be able to identify those abbreviations that have been determined to be dangerous due to their potential for misinterpretation.

Recommendations for Focused Study

1. *The Book of Style for Medical Transcription, 3rd Edition*
2. Chapter 9: Section 9.3
3. *The Book of Style 3rd Edition Workbook*
   Chapter 9
4. The Joint Commission website (www.jointcomission.org)
   Standards/National Patient Safety Goals
5. The Institute for Safe Medication Practices website (www.ismp.org)
   Error-Prone Abbreviations List

Sample Questions

Each question below represents the kind of format and content, per the exam blue print, that an RMT candidate can expect to find on the RMT exam. *Note: These are sample questions only. They are questions that do not currently appear on the RMT exam. Though some may represent items retired from previous exam forms, not all items have been psychometrically analyzed, and AHDI cautions candidates against the presumption that these items alone may be diagnostic or indicative of candidate performance.* (**Answer key at end of chapter.)**

5. Which abbreviation appears on the Joint Commission list of dangerous abbreviations?

    A. gtt
    B. q.i.d.
    C. q.o.d.
    D. q.a.m.

6. The Joint Commission recommends that organizations identify three abbreviations in addition to the basic *Do Not Use* list that will be considered dangerous to use. What is one term that organizations might select for addition to their *Do Not Use* list?

    A. q.i.d.
    B. mL
    C. D/C
    D. a.c.

Sample Questions Answer Key

1. D
2. B
3. A
4. B
5. C
6. C

Numbers and Numeric Referents

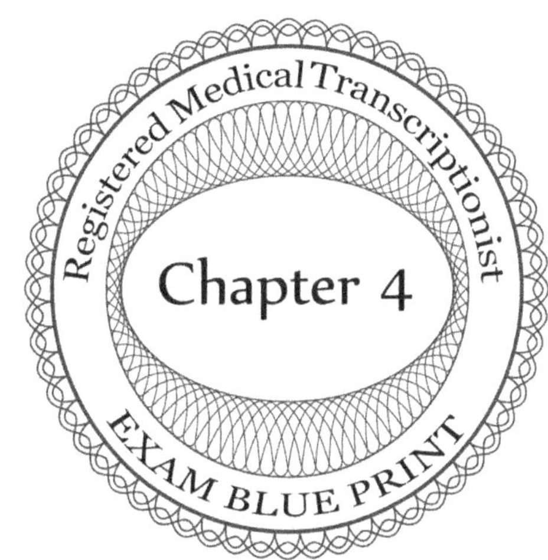

"There is arguably no more critical information recorded and relied upon than the numeric values that represent a wide variety of indicators for both cause and effect in managing disease...numbers are a critical part of the patient record."

– The Book of Style for Medical Transcription, 3e

Chapter Overview

Numbers are at the heart of medicine. Diagnosis and care of patients, reimbursement for medical services, and the creation of information for scientific study are all dependent upon a world of quantified data. The data include measurements of time, amounts, frequencies, relationships, and also encompass standard expressions of classification. Clearly an error in a numerical datum or in the exchange of clinical information can compromise any or all of these functions of the clinical document. One small quantitative error can have disproportionately large effects upon the integrity of healthcare documentation, and likewise, one small error in the communication of quantitative data can compromise patient care and safety, alter the level of reimbursement, or distort scientific findings. The medical transcriptionist, though not required to be a professional mathematician or statistician, must have a solid understanding of the meaning of quantitative data in healthcare documents and of the correct expression of numerical information.

The body of knowledge for medical transcriptionists therefore includes an understanding of:

- The correct expression of numbers.

- The correct usage of numerical expressions in various clinical contexts.
- The various expressions of time.
- The appropriate use of arabic and roman numerals in clinical documents.
- The correct expression of percentages, proportions, and ranges in clinical documents.
- The correct uses and expression of standard and metric units of measure.

There are **7 objectives**[1] on the RMT blue print that address concepts related to these domains and against which an RMT exam candidate will be evaluated. In this chapter, we will walk through each objective listed under *RMT Blue Print Section 1: Transcription Standards of Style* that relate to these domains.

Objectives 1.26 and 1.27

Objective 1.26: *Given numeric values or sentences containing numeric values, identify the one that reflects correct expression of a number or numbers.*

Objective 1.27: *Given a sentence where the numeric value is a blank, identify the correct numeric expression to fill in the blank, or given a dictated word, phrase, or sentence containing a numeric value, identify the correctly transcribed expression of a numeric value.*

Rationale

As in most areas of medical information, in the realm of numeric expression there are agreed-upon standards of expression in various contexts. To promote the accurate communication of numbers in healthcare documentation, the medical transcriptionist must be aware of, and able to apply correctly, the rules (and exceptions to rules) that govern the written expression of numbers in clinical contexts, including the appropriate use of punctuation with numerical expressions.

---

[1] Objectives 1.30, 1.32, and 1.35 on the RMT blue print are audio objectives that also relate to Numbers and Numeric Referents. Look for blue print guidance on audio objectives in upcoming AHDI exam prep products.

Recommendations for Focused Study

1. *The Book of Style for Medical Transcription, 3rd Edition*
   Chapter 10
2. *The Book of Style 3rd Edition Workbook*
   Chapter 10
3. *The AMA Manual of Style, 10th Edition*
   Section 4, Chapter 19

Sample Questions

Each question below represents the kind of format and content, per the exam blue print, that an RMT candidate can expect to find on the RMT exam. *Note: These are sample questions only. They are questions that do not currently appear on the RMT exam. Though some may represent items retired from previous exam forms, not all items have been psychometrically analyzed, and AHDI cautions candidates against the presumption that these items alone may be diagnostic or indicative of candidate performance.* **(Answer key at end of chapter.)**

1. Which sentence reflects a correctly expressed number?

   A. The patient is in her 40's.
   B. The patient is in her forties.
   C. The patient is in her 40s.
   D. The patient is in her forties'.

2. Which phrase correctly combines numerals with words?

   A. In 1997 there were 1.8 thousand cases of malaria in the US
   B. There are between 1 and 2 million deaths from malaria yearly in Africa.
   C. One treatment regimen for malaria consists of 2 100 mg tablets of Proguanil daily.
   D. Malaria may be treated using 2 one-hundred milligram tablets of Proguanil daily.

3. **The patient had a corneal laceration at ____________.**

   Which is the appropriate expression for the blank above?

A. 9:00
B. nine o'clock
C. 9 o'clock
D. the 9-o'clock position

4. **We inserted a three five K wire.**

What is the correct transcription of the above dictated sentence?

A. We inserted a 3.5 K wire.
B. We inserted a 3.50 K wire.
C. We inserted a 0.035 K wire.
D. We inserted a .35 K wire.

Objective 1.28

Objective 1.28: *Given military time, identify the equivalent standard time, or given a standard time, identify the equivalent military time.*

Rationale

Military time, the 24-hour clock, and various correct forms for the expression of time are essential elements in the medical transcriptionist's knowledge. Healthcare providers, both in the US and internationally, often use the 24-hour system in clinical documentation, and the transcriptionist must understand the relationship between that system and the standard a.m. and p.m. designations.

Recommendations for Focused Study

1. *The Book of Style for Medical Transcription, 3rd Edition*
   Chapter 10: Section 10.3.13
2. *The Book of Style 3rd Edition Workbook*
   Chapter 10
3. *The AMA Manual of Style, 10th Edition*
   Section 4, Chapter 19

Sample Questions

Each question below represents the kind of format and content, per the exam blue print, that an RMT candidate can expect to find on the RMT exam. *Note: These are sample questions only. They are questions that do not currently appear on the RMT exam. Though some may represent items retired from previous exam forms, not all items have been psychometrically analyzed, and AHDI cautions candidates against the presumption that these items alone may be diagnostic or indicative of candidate performance.* **(Answer key at end of chapter.)**

5. The patient was admitted at 1900 hours; what is the equivalent expression in standard time?

   A. 7 a.m.
   B. 7 p.m.
   C. 9 a.m.
   D. 9 p.m.

6. What is the equivalent, in military time, of 11 a.m.?

   A. 1100 hours
   B. 2100 hours
   C. 2300 hours
   D. 0100 hours

Objective 1.29

Objective 1.29: *Given numeric expressions, identify whether a roman numeral or an arabic numeral is required.*

Rationale

Conventions of expression govern the use of arabic or roman numerals in healthcare documentation. To ensure clear and accurate written communication, the medical transcriptionist must understand the correct usages of these numerals in varying contexts such as classification systems.

Recommendations for Focused Study

1. *The Book of Style for Medical Transcription, 3rd Edition*
   Chapter 10: Sections 10.1.2 and 14.3
2. *The Book of Style 3rd Edition Workbook*
   Chapter 10

Sample Questions

Each question below represents the kind of format and content, per the exam blue print, that an RMT candidate can expect to find on the RMT exam. *Note: These are sample questions only. They are questions that do not currently appear on the RMT exam. Though some may represent items retired from previous exam forms, not all items have been psychometrically analyzed, and AHDI cautions candidates against the presumption that these items alone may be diagnostic or indicative of candidate performance.* **(Answer key at end of chapter.)**

7. For which expression are roman numerals required?

   A. Psychiatric axis diagnoses
   B. Diabetes type
   C. Cervical intraepithelial neoplasia grade
   D. TNM cancer staging system

8. Which phrase is correctly transcribed?

   A. Mallampati-Samsoon class II
   B. LeFort 1 fracture
   C. Salter-Harris 2 fracture
   D. Histology showing a grade III tumor

Objective 1.31

Objective 1.31: *Given sentences, identify the one containing the correct expression of a percent, proportion, ratio, or numeric range, or given a dictated excerpt containing an underlined proportion or range, identify the correctly transcribed expression.*

Rationale

Percentages, proportions, ratios, ranges, and other expressions of numeric relationships are very basic to clinical and scientific medicine. But the meaning of these numbers, and the accurate communication of that meaning, absolutely depends upon the correct expression of these relationships in written documents. Therefore, the medical transcriptionist or editor, partnering with healthcare providers, ensures that the written numerical expressions accurately convey the meaning intended.

Recommendations for Focused Study

1. *The Book of Style for Medical Transcription, 3rd Edition*
   Chapter 11
2. *The Book of Style 3rd Edition Workbook*
   Chapter 11
3. *The AMA Manual of Style, 10th Edition*
   Section 4, Chapter 19

Sample Questions

Each question below represents the kind of format and content, per the exam blue print, that an RMT candidate can expect to find on the RMT exam. *Note: These are sample questions only. They are questions that do not currently appear on the RMT exam. Though some may represent items retired from previous exam forms, not all items have been psychometrically analyzed, and AHDI cautions candidates against the presumption that these items alone may be diagnostic or indicative of candidate performance.* (**Answer key at end of chapter.)**

9. Which sentence is correctly transcribed?

   A. The incidence of infection is 0.5%.
   B. The incidence of infection is .5%.
   C. The incidence of infection is half of one percent.
   D. The incidence of infection is 0.50 percent.

10. Which range is correctly expressed?

A. The range of values is from 0.5-1%.
B. The range of values is from 0.5 to 1%.
C. The range of values is from 0.5% to 1%.
D. The range of values is from one to five percent.

Objectives 1.33 and 1.34

Objective 1.33: *Given a metric unit, identify the property it measures, or given a property, identify the metric unit by which it is measured, or given sentences, identify the one that represents correct expression of a metric or standard unit of measure.*

Objective 1.34: *Given a sentence where the numeric value is blank, identify the correct expression of the numeric value and unit of measure.*

Rationale

The vast range of numeric values in medicine includes various units of measurement appropriate to specific contexts, and the medical transcriptionist must know what unit of measurement is appropriate in which context as well as the correct written expression of those units of measurement. The correct specification of units of measure completes the meaning of measurements in healthcare documentation. Although much of the world uses metric measurements, many United States healthcare providers continue to employ the standard English system (feet, inches, pounds, etc), and the medical transcriptionist should understand both systems.

Recommendations for Focused Study

1. *The Book of Style for Medical Transcription, 3rd Edition*
   Chapter 12
2. *The Book of Style 3rd Edition Workbook*
   Chapter 12

Sample Questions

Each question below represents the kind of format and content, per the exam blue print, that an RMT candidate can expect to find on the RMT exam. *Note: These are sample questions only. They are questions that* do not *currently appear on the RMT exam. Though some may represent items retired from previous exam forms, not all items have been psychometrically analyzed, and AHDI cautions candidates against the presumption that these items alone may be diagnostic or indicative of candidate performance.* (**Answer key at end of chapter.)**

11. Which item shows the correct expression of a unit of measure?

    A. The incision was 3 mmol.
    B. The lesion measured 2.5 x 4 mL.
    C. Baby's birth weight was 8 lbs 6 oz.
    D. The patient was given a 2 L bolus of normal saline.

12. The metric unit of ampere is used to measure what property?

    A. Time
    B. Electric current
    C. Amount of substance
    D. Mass

13. **The laceration was _________.**

    Which is the correct expression for the blank above?

    A. 2.5 in
    B. 2.5 cm
    C. 2-1/2 in
    D. 2.5-cm

14. **The baby's weight was ________.**

    Which value is correctly expressed for the blank above?

    A. 3.591 kilograms
    B. 3591 g
    C. 6 lbs 14.7 oz
    D. 3591 mL

Sample Questions Answer Key

1. C
2. A
3. D
4. C
5. B
6. A
7. A
8. A
9. A
10. C
11. D
12. B
13. B
14. B

Section 2

Clinical Medicine

"I have been credentialed since 1994. I have done so for myself as I am a healthcare professional. I have attended every ACE, from Las Vegas to Austin. I became a chapter president even though I do not like public speaking and never thought I would do that, as President of the Granite State Chapter in New Hampshire. If we don't think we have self-worth in this profession – that we just type or we just read and correct errors – and not become credentialed, our employers will agree with that sentiment and credentialing will not mean anything. There is power in numbers. It is important to become credentialed. Do it for yourself." – Darlene Marie Jacobs, CMT

Medical Terminology

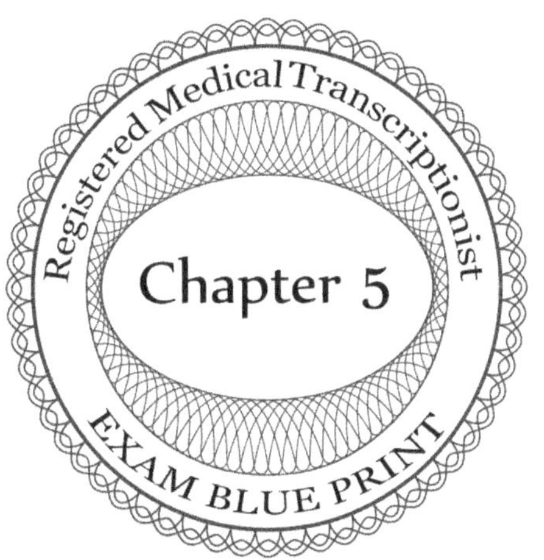

"Every profession has a range of special terms used by practitioners in that field. When learning medical language, you are learning much more than just words—you are learning fundamental concepts about the body in health and disease and about common medical problems."[1]

– Stedman's Medical Terminology: Steps to Success in Medical Language

Chapter Overview

The language of medicine is complex, rooted in history, and highly specialized. There is almost no end to the process of learning medical terminology, because the vocabulary and syntax of medical language evolve through time, moving with changing concepts of disease and treatment, and changing as new technologies emerge and older technologies fall by the wayside. In fact, for many medical transcriptionists, the ever-evolving nature of medical language can be both the most fascinating and most challenging aspect of their work. The beginning practitioner must command a basic understanding of how medical terms are formulated, the meanings of basic terms common in clinical medicine (including the intriguing terms that comprise medical homonyms and synonyms), and terminology used in anatomical description. This is the foundation upon which a new RMT will need to build a more in-depth understanding of clinical language and the diagnostic process. Without these fundamentals, an MT will struggle to understand the breadth and scope of what he or she is hearing in the narrative, which puts the MT at risk for error and undermines the goal of providing risk management support to health care.

---

[1] Creason, Charlotte, ed. "Why Use Medical Terminology?" *Stedman's Medical Terminology: Steps to Success in Medical Language* Philadelphia: Lippincott Williams & Wilkins, 2011. 2.

The body of knowledge for medical transcriptionists therefore includes an understanding of:

- How medical terms are built using prefixes, suffixes, root words, and combining forms.
- The meaning of basic and essential terms in the general vocabulary of clinical medicine.
- The correct meaning and spelling of homonyms and synonyms in medicine.
- The concepts and terms used to categorize and describe anatomical position and planes that identify the location of organs and organ systems in the human body.

There are **4 objectives** on the RMT blue print that address concepts related to these domains and against which an RMT exam candidate will be evaluated. In this chapter, we will walk through each objective listed under *RMT Blue Print Section 2: Clinical Medicine* that relate to these domains.

Objective 2.1

Objective 2.1: *Given the meaning of a word, identify the correct prefix, suffix, combining word, or root word, or given a prefix, suffix or combining form, and a definition, identify what is needed to create another given word.*

Rationale

Medical terms, however complex, can be broken down into component parts: root word, prefixes, and suffixes. The medical transcriptionist who understands the construction and meanings of these elements, individually, will be well-equipped to understand the accurate use and spelling of medical terminology, and will have a sound basis for beginning to understand even unfamiliar or new terms. This knowledge of the "bones" of terminology is a basic, essential tool for medical transcriptionists at all levels throughout their careers.

Recommendations for Focused Study

1. *The Language of Medicine, 9th Edition* (Saunders)
   Chapters 1-4
2. *Stedman's Medical Terminology: Steps to Success in Medical Language* (Wolters Kluwer)
   Chapters 2, 4-16
3. *Medical Transcription Fundamentals: Where Success Takes Root* (Wolters Kluwer)
   Chapter 3
4. *The Medical Transcription Workbook, 3rd edition* (Health Professions Institute)
   Section 2

Sample Questions

Each question below represents the kind of format and content, per the exam blue print, that an RMT candidate can expect to find on the RMT exam. *Note: These are sample questions only. They are questions that do not currently appear on the RMT exam. Though some may represent items retired from previous exam forms, not all items have been psychometrically analyzed, and AHDI cautions candidates against the presumption that these items alone may be diagnostic or indicative of candidate performance.* **(Answer key at end of chapter.)**

1. Given the prefix "leuko-," what must be added to create the word meaning *a decrease in the number of white blood cells*?

   A. –emia
   B. –coria
   C. –penia
   D. –malacia

2. What medical term is formed by combining the term for the noncellular portion of the circulating blood with the suffix meaning withdrawal?

   A. hemolysis
   B. plasmapheresis
   C. hematophagia
   D. plasmorrhexis

3. Which refers to a *blue* condition?

   A. erythema
   B. leukoplakia
   C. eosinophilia
   D. cyanosis

Objective 2.2

Objective 2.2: *Given a medical term, identify the definition, or given a definition, identify the correct medical term.*

Rationale

The vast range of medical terminology is not acquired overnight but rather step by step as the medical transcriptionist grows from student to level 1 practitioner and beyond. The first step will involve acquisition of a vocabulary of basic terms, those commonly used in general practice and family practice, and in basic report types such as SOAP notes and the history and physical examination. These terms become familiar through study and repeated use, and will give the medical transcriptionist a firm foundation for work as a level 1 practitioner.

Recommendations for Focused Study

1. *The Language of Medicine, 9th Edition* (Saunders)
   Chapters 3-22
2. *Stedman's Medical Terminology: Steps to Success in Medical Language* (Wolters Kluwer)
   Chapters 2-16
3. *Medical Transcription Fundamentals: Where Success Takes Root* (Wolters Kluwer)
   Chapters 7-19
4. *The Medical Transcription Workbook, 3rd edition* (Health Professions Institute)
   Section 2
5. *Stedman's Medical Terminology Flash Cards*

Sample Questions

Each question below represents the kind of format and content, per the exam blue print, that an RMT candidate can expect to find on the RMT exam. *Note: These are sample questions only. They are questions that do not currently appear on the RMT exam. Though some may represent items retired from previous exam forms, not all items have been psychometrically analyzed, and AHDI cautions candidates against the presumption that these items alone may be diagnostic or indicative of candidate performance.* (**Answer key at end of chapter.)**

4. Which term describes the dimpling of skin in a breast cancer patient?

   A. peaux d'orange
   B. pou dorange
   C. peau d'orange
   D. peau dorange

5. Which term describes a therapeutic immersion of the patient's hips and buttocks in liquid?

   A. a Sits bath
   B. a sitz bath
   C. a Sitz bath
   D. a sittz bath

Objective 2.3

Objective 2.3: *Given sentences, identify the correct use of a medical term commonly confused for another.*

Rationale

Terms that sound alike but have different meanings will be a career-long challenge for the medical transcriptionist. The words in question will be spelled differently but sound so similar that they are easily confused for one another. In these situations, it will often be the responsibility of the medical transcriptionist to decipher precise meaning, based on context, in order to determine the correct spelling to use and to accurately convey what the healthcare provider intended to say. Synonyms, on the other hand, are words that share meaning, contribute flexibility and variety to medical language. Here, the role of the medical transcription practitioner is to understand the accurate use of synonymous terms and to assist (as always) the healthcare provider in creating a document that is clear, reliable, and readable. The medical transcriptionist at any level of expertise must also be able to make good judgments about when the provider must be queried to clarify meaning. There is no guessing in medical transcription!

Recommendations for Focused Study

1. *The Medical Transcription Workbook, 3rd Edition* (Health Professions Institute)
   Section 1: Spelling and Usage
2. *The Book of Style for Medical Transcription, 3rd Edition*
   Appendix C: Usage Glossary

Sample Questions

Each question below represents the kind of format and content, per the exam blue print, that an RMT candidate can expect to find on the RMT exam. *Note: These are sample questions only. They are questions that do not currently appear on the RMT exam. Though some may represent items retired from previous exam forms, not all items have been psychometrically analyzed, and AHDI cautions candidates against the presumption that these items alone may be diagnostic or indicative of candidate performance.* **(Answer key at end of chapter.)**

6. Which represents the correct use of a medical term commonly confused for another?

   A. She describes her dysphagia as the sensation of having something stuck in her throat.
   B. KUB revealed right-sided urethral dilatation.
   C. We diagnosed the child with serious otitis media after examination of the left ear revealed significant fluid.
   D. Gross inspection of the appendix revealed it to be full of thecal stones.

7. Which statement reflects the correct location of the nerve?

   A. Peroneal nerve dysfunction led to loss of sensation in the foot.
   B. Peroneal nerve dysfunction led to loss of function in the thumb.

C. Peroneal nerve dysfunction led to loss of sensation in the pelvis.
D. Peroneal nerve dysfunction led to loss of function in the shoulder.

Objective 2.4

Objective 2.4: *Given a directional term, an anatomical position term, or a body plane term, identify the correct definition, or given a definition, identify the correct directional term, the correct anatomical position term, or the correct body plane term.*

Rationale

The human body, a unified entity, is conceptually divided into directional relationships and planes, for purposes of localizing organs and systems involved in both normal and pathologic processes. The level 1 medical transcription practitioner must understand these basic divisions and categories, which will often serve to clarify word meanings and usage as well as provide essential information for diagnosis and treatment. This knowledge is the basis for understanding human anatomy and physiology, which is essential to accurate and clear transcription of clinical information.

Recommendations for Focused Study

1. *The Language of Medicine, 9th Edition* (Saunders)
   Chapters 2, 5, 7-17
2. *Stedman's Medical Terminology: Steps to Success in Medical Language* (Wolters Kluwer)
   Chapter 3
3. *Medical Transcription Fundamentals: Where Success Takes Root* (Wolters Kluwer)
   Chapter 3
4. *The Medical Transcription Workbook, 3rd Edition* (Health Professions Institute)
   Section 2
5. *Stedman's Medical Terminology Flash Cards*

Sample Questions

Each question below represents the kind of format and content, per the exam blue print, that an RMT candidate can expect to find on the RMT exam. *Note: These are* *sample questions only. They are questions that <u>do not</u> currently appear on the RMT exam. Though some may represent items retired from previous exam forms, not all items have been psychometrically analyzed, and AHDI cautions candidates against the presumption that these items alone may be diagnostic or indicative of candidate performance.* **(Answer key at end of chapter.)**

8. In the upper extremity, what bones are distal to the metacarpals?

   A. carpals
   B. phalanges
   C. cuboid and talus
   D. hamate and [illegible]

9. Where is the stomach located in relation to the heart?

   A. lateral
   B. medial
   C. anterior
   D. posterior

10. The diaphragm divides which two body cavities?

   A. cranial and spinal
   B. spinal and thoracic
   C. thoracic and abdominal
   D. abdominal and pelvic

Sample Questions Answer Key

1. C
2. B
3. D
4. C
5. B
6. A
7. A
8. B
9. C
10. C

Clinical Diagnostics

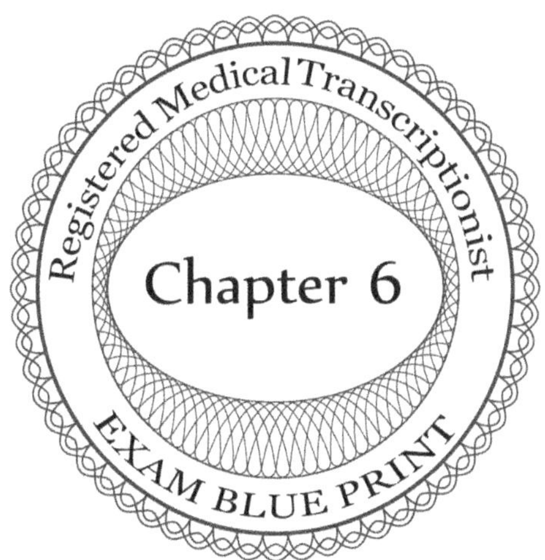

"Medical diagnosis is the process by which a physician seeks to learn the nature, cause, and extent of an illness, injury, or congenital or developmental disorder. Obviously at least some tentative or general notion of what is wrong must precede any rational effort to treat it."[1]

– Laboratory Tests and Diagnostic Procedures in Medicine

Chapter Overview

The diagnosis of diseases and conditions and the practice of evidence-based medicine are dependent upon the use of objective diagnostic tools found in the realm of the medical laboratory and the discipline of radiology. Samples of body materials, tissues, and fluids analyzed in the laboratory reveal the state of an individual's health and the presence or absence of specific pathologies. Diagnostic imaging examinations, using increasingly sophisticated technologies, offer the clinician the ability to see inside the body in order to diagnose and treat the patient. Because the laboratory and the diagnostic imaging or radiology department are so closely related to everyday clinical practice, the medical transcriptionist must have an understanding of the terminologies and methods used in these areas. As is true for other aspects of modern medicine, the field of knowledge is virtually unlimited, and the transcriptionist will continually acquire new knowledge about these terminologies. As a new practitioner, the level 1 MT will be familiar with the kinds of laboratory and radiologic diagnostic studies commonly performed in the outpatient

---

[1] Dirckx, John H. MD. *Laboratory Tests & Diagnostic Procedures in Medicine.* Modesto: Health Professions Institute, 2004.

setting either as tools of routine assessment or as diagnosis and treatment for commonly occurring conditions.

The body of knowledge for Level 1 medical transcriptionists therefore includes an understanding of:

- Commonly used laboratory panels, their constituent tests and the purposes for which they are used.
- The normal values in commonly used laboratory studies.
- The types of imaging studies, and the purposes for which they are used.
- The terminology and abbreviations associated with common diagnostic imaging studies.

There are **5 objectives**[2] on the RMT blue print that address concepts related to these domains and against which an RMT exam candidate will be evaluated. In this chapter, we will walk through each objective listed under *RMT Blue Print Section 2: Clinical Medicine* that relate to these domains.

Objectives 2.6, 2.7, and 2.25

Objective 2.6: *Given a laboratory panel, identify the tests associated with that panel or identify the tests that are part of a laboratory panel.*

Objective 2.7: *Given a laboratory test, identify the normal values, or given a laboratory result, identify if the value is low, high, or normal.*

Objective 2.25: *Given a diagnostic test, including laboratory studies, identify what is being measured.*

Rationale

As a partner in the creation of accurate and reliable healthcare documentation, the medical transcriptionist and editor will be able to monitor the record for the correct

---

[2] Objectives 2.8, 2.11, and 2.26 on the blue print are audio objectives that also relate to the Clinical Diagnostics. Look for blue print guidance on audio objectives in upcoming AHDI exam prep products.

description of laboratory tests and their results. A hurried healthcare provider can all-too-easily misspeak laboratory descriptions or results, describe as normal a test result usually considered abnormal, or make incorrect choices from a drop-down menu in an electronic health record. The transcription practitioner who understands the meaning and appropriate context of laboratory tests can perform an important quality-assurance function at the point of creation of the permanent healthcare record.

Recommendations for Focused Study

1. *The Language of Medicine, 9th Edition* (Saunders)
   Laboratory Tests, Clinical Procedures, and Abbreviations – Chapters 5-19
2. *Stedman's Medical Terminology: Steps to Success in Medical Language* (Wolters Kluwer)
   Tests and Procedures – Chapters 4-16; Appendix C
3. *Medical Transcription Fundamentals: Where Success Takes Root* (Wolters Kluwer)
   Chapter 6; Diagnostic Studies and Procedures – Chapters 7-19
4. *The Medical Transcription Workbook, 3rd Edition* (Health Professions Institute)
   Section 2
5. *The Book of Style for Medical Transcription, 3rd Edition*
   Measurement & Quantitation – Section 3
6. *Laboratory Tests & Diagnostic Procedures in Medicine* (Health Professions Institute)
   Chapters 5-15

Sample Questions

Each question below represents the kind of format and content, per the exam blue print, that an RMT candidate can expect to find on the RMT exam. *Note: These are sample questions only. They are questions that do not currently appear on the RMT exam. Though some may represent items retired from previous exam forms, not all items have been psychometrically analyzed, and AHDI cautions candidates against the presumption that these items alone may be diagnostic or indicative of candidate performance.* **(Answer key at end of chapter.)**

1. Which test is included in a basic metabolic panel?

   A. PSA
   B. CRP
   C. calcium
   D. cholesterol

2. What organ function is assessed using the BUN and creatinine tests?

   A. liver
   B. kidney
   C. pancreas
   D. gallbladder

3. Which of the following laboratory tests would be associated with the term *differential*?

   A. urinalysis
   B. thyroid panel
   C. morphology study
   D. complete blood count

4. What does a Gram stain evaluate?

   A. Cellular organelles.
   B. Shape and size of red blood cells.
   C. Number of eosinophils counted per high-power field.
   D. Presence of certain infectious organisms in a specimen.

5. Which of the following potassium levels would indicate normal renal function?

   A. 4 mEq/L
   B. 12 mEq/L
   C. 20 mEq/L
   D. 2 mEq/L

6. Which serum sodium value is within the normal range?

   A. 1240 mEq/L
   B. 240 mEq/L
   C. 140 mEq/L
   D. 39 mEq/L

Objectives 2.9 and 2.10

Objective 2.9: *Given an imaging study type, identify the use or definition of that study type.*

Objective 2.10: *Given an imaging study, identify common abbreviations and terminology associated with that study.*

Rationale

In their role as de facto quality assessors of the clinical document, medical transcriptionists must have a fund of knowledge about diagnostic image modalities and their uses. Even if an MT moves out of the classroom into the workplace and never transcribes in radiology specifically, reference to imaging study findings will be encountered in nearly every clinical setting, whether outpatient or acute care. Therefore, a job-ready RMT will have a basic understanding of the technologies used in diagnostic imaging studies and a thorough knowledge of the terminology used in connection with each type of study, including commonly used abbreviations.

Recommendations for Focused Study

1. *The Language of Medicine, 9th Edition* (Saunders)
   Laboratory Tests, Clinical Procedures, and Abbreviations – Chapters 5-19
   Radiology, Nuclear Medicine, and Radiation Therapy – Chapter 20
2. *Stedman's Medical Terminology: Steps to Success in Medical Language* (Wolters Kluwer)
   Tests and Procedures – Chapters 4-16
3. *Medical Transcription Fundamentals: Where Success Takes Root* (Wolters Kluwer)
   Chapter 8 – Laboratory Studies and Medical Imaging; Chapters 7-19

4. *The Medical Transcription Workbook, 3rd Edition* (Health Professions Institute)
   Section 2
5. *The Book of Style for Medical Transcription, 3rd Edition*
   Chapter 24 – Section 24.1
6. *Laboratory Tests & Diagnostic Procedures in Medicine* (Health Professions Institute)
   Chapters 16-24

Sample Questions

Each question below represents the kind of format and content, per the exam blue print, that an RMT candidate can expect to find on the RMT exam. *Note: These are sample questions only. They are questions that do not currently appear on the RMT exam. Though some may represent items retired from previous exam forms, not all items have been psychometrically analyzed, and AHDI cautions candidates against the presumption that these items alone may be diagnostic or indicative of candidate performance.* (**Answer key at end of chapter.)**

7. Which statement is true of an MRI study?

   A. It uses a small dose of ionizing radiation.
   B. It measures the emission of gamma rays.
   C. It exposes the body to high-frequency sound waves.
   D. It polarizes the nuclei of hydrogen atoms.

8. Which condition might be detected on a myelogram?

   A. leukemia
   B. diverticulitis
   C. spinal stenosis
   D. aortic aneurysm

9. On what kind of imaging study will *T2 images* be obtained?

   A. MRI
   B. CAT
   C. EEG
   D. DEXA

10. The phrase *PA and lateral* refers to beam positioning for which radiographic study?

    A. sinus series
    B. KUB
    C. lumbar spine films
    D. chest x-ray

Sample Questions Answer Key

1. C
2. B
3. D
4. D
5. A
6. C
7. D
8. C
9. A
10. D

Pharmacology

"Pharmacology is a fascinating and multifaceted discipline that impacts not only our professional careers but our personal lives as well. From our role as members of the healthcare team to that of consumers, pharmacology plays a part in our lives."

– Understanding Pharmacology for Health Professionals[1]

Chapter Overview

The area of medical practice known as pharmacology is based on the confluence of the facts of physical and organic chemistry with the realities of human anatomy and physiology. And pharmacology is also big business; some of the rules about transcription of pharmacologic terms reflect the legal aspects of drug creation and patenting. Because of the critical role of drugs in the treatment of human pathologies, an understanding of the basics of pharmacology is of central importance in the accurate transcription of healthcare records. This in turn requires the incorporation of some basic knowledge of chemistry into the transcriptionist's fund of knowledge. An understanding of the range of possibilities for drug dosages and regimens will also be basic required knowledge. Here, once again, we see the potential for medical transcriptionists to act as first-line quality assessors, monitoring the record during the process of creation for accurate descriptions of drug quantities, routes of administration, and dosing schedules.

---

[1] Turley, Susan M. *Understanding Pharmacology for Health Professionals.* New Jersey: Prentice Hall, Inc., 2010.

The body of knowledge for Level 1 medical transcriptionists therefore includes an understanding of:

- The appropriate routes of drug administration for various drugs and drug types.
- The basic terminology pertaining to pharmaceuticals, including definitions of commonly used drugs and associated vocabulary.
- The relationship between generic and brand names for commonly used drugs.
- Pharmaceutical categories.
- Names of drugs used in treatment of more commonly occurring conditions.

There are **5 objectives**[2] on the RMT blue print that address concepts related to these domains and against which an RMT exam candidate will be evaluated. In this chapter, we will walk through each objective listed under *RMT Blue Print Section 2: Clinical Medicine* that relate to these domains.

Objective 2.12

Objective 2.12: *Given a drug or drug type, identify the route or form of administration, or given a route or form of administration, identify the drug or drug type.*

Rationale

A medical transcriptionist who understands the routes of administration for various drugs brings to the transcription task an enhanced ability to understand the healthcare provider's intentions in creating a clinical record. Such knowledge not only assists the transcription practitioner to interpret dictation that may be less than perfectly clear, but also allows the practitioner to ensure that statements about the route and form of drug administration are accurate and accurately recorded.

---

[2] Objective 2.16 on the RMT blue print is an audio objective that also relates to Pharmacology. Look for blue print guidance on audio objectives in upcoming AHDI exam prep products.

Recommendations for Focused Study

1. *The Book of Style for Medical Transcription, 3rd Edition*
   Chapter 13
2. *Understanding Pharmacology for Health Professionals, 4th Edition* (Prentice Hall)
   Chapter 3
3. *The Language of Medicine, 9th Edition* (Saunders)
   Chapter 21

Sample Questions

Each question below represents the kind of format and content, per the exam blue print, that an RMT candidate can expect to find on the RMT exam. *Note: These are sample questions only. They are questions that do not currently appear on the RMT exam. Though some may represent items retired from previous exam forms, not all items have been psychometrically analyzed, and AHDI cautions candidates against the presumption that these items alone may be diagnostic or indicative of candidate performance.* **(Answer key at end of chapter.)**

1. Anticholinergics, like *Atrovent*, can only be administered via which route?

   A. oral
   B. intravenous
   C. inhalation
   D. transdermal

2. Which of the following drugs, used to stimulate red blood cells in chemotherapy patients, is given intravenously?

   A. Keflex
   B. Epogen
   C. Nexium
   D. Remicade

Objective 2.13

Objective 2.13: *Given a drug term, identify the definition, or given a definition of a drug term, identify the term.*

Rationale

The level 1 medical transcriptionist is embarking on a life-long learning process, and this is particularly true in the pharmaceutical field of knowledge, where change is a constant. However, there are basic drug terms and definitions that should form part of the available vocabulary of the beginning practitioner; these would include frequently encountered terms pertaining to family practice and outpatient treatment.

Recommendations for Focused Study

1. *The Book of Style for Medical Transcription, 3rd Edition*
   Chapter 13
2. *Understanding Pharmacology for Health Professionals, 4th Edition* (Prentice Hall)
   Chapters 7-24
3. *The Language of Medicine, 9th Edition* (Saunders)
   Chapter 21

Sample Questions

Each question below represents the kind of format and content, per the exam blue print, that an RMT candidate can expect to find on the RMT exam. *Note: These are sample questions only. They are questions that do not currently appear on the RMT exam. Though some may represent items retired from previous exam forms, not all items have been psychometrically analyzed, and AHDI cautions candidates against the presumption that these items alone may be diagnostic or indicative of candidate performance.* (**Answer key at end of chapter.)**

3. Which of the following terms denotes a class of drugs used in treating hypertension?

   A. viricides
   B. diuretics

C. ergotamines
D. phenothiazines

4. Which of the following terms is defined as a rapidly developing reaction to a drug that includes symptoms such as swelling of lips and tongue, or even death?

A. analgesia
B. anconitis
C. anaphylaxis
D. anoxia

Objectives 2.14 and 2.15

Objective 2.14: *Given a drug's generic name, identify the brand name, or given a drug's brand name, identify the generic name.*

Objective 2.15: *Given a drug, identify the pharmacological category.*

Rationale

For most drugs, a period of patent protection for a brand name will be eventually succeeded by the availability of a generic version of the same pharmaceutical product. It often happens that both brand name and generic versions of a given drug will be in common use in clinical practice. To ensure clarity and accuracy of communication, the medical transcriptionist will know the relevant terms for both the branded and generic forms of the drug. Likewise, an understanding of the ways drugs are categorized will enhance the transcriptionist's ability to interpret dictation and create an accurate record that reflects the healthcare provider's intended meaning. At a level 1 of transcription practice, the scope of knowledge will include drugs commonly prescribed in routine maintenance and outpatient care.

Recommendations for Focused Study

1. *The Book of Style for Medical Transcription, 3rd Edition*
   Chapter 13

2. *Understanding Pharmacology for Health Professionals, 4th Edition* (Prentice Hall)
   Chapters 2 and 4
3. *The Language of Medicine, 9th Edition* (Saunders)
   Chapter 21

Sample Questions

Each question below represents the kind of format and content, per the exam blue print, that an RMT candidate can expect to find on the RMT exam. *Note: These are sample questions only. They are questions that do not currently appear on the RMT exam. Though some may represent items retired from previous exam forms, not all items have been psychometrically analyzed, and AHDI cautions candidates against the presumption that these items alone may be diagnostic or indicative of candidate performance.* (**Answer key at end of chapter.)**

5. What generic drug has the brand name Nexium?

   A. lisinopril
   B. esomeprazole
   C. clopidogrel
   D. clindamycin

6. Which is the brand name for levofloxacin?

   A. Levaquin
   B. Levsin
   C. Lovenox
   D. Lupron

7. Which of the following drugs is an amebicide?

   A. Cervidil
   B. Benadryl
   C. Flagyl
   D. Feldene

8. To what pharmacological category does aspirin belong?

   A. PPI
   B. NSAID
   C. SSRI
   D. HRT

Objective 2.27

Objective 2.27: *Given a medication, identify the symptom or disease for which it is prescribed, or given a symptom or disease, identify the medication that is prescribed.*

Rationale

The healthcare provider is ultimately responsible for the accuracy of clinical documentation, but the knowledgeable medical transcriptionist has a significant role to play in the creation of accurate documents. Knowledge of the purposes of specific drugs and their uses in treatment will facilitate correct interpretation of dictation and enable the transcriptionist or editor to monitor the accuracy of the document. With wide adoption of the EHR, speech-recognized reports, and structured data entry, errors in description of pharmaceutical treatments can be replicated and perpetuated throughout a record, and may prove difficult to correct. The knowledgeable medical transcriptionist can be a first line of defense against such scenarios.

Recommendations for Focused Study

1. *The Book of Style for Medical Transcription, 3rd Edition*
   Chapter 13
2. *Understanding Pharmacology for Health Professionals, 4th Edition* (Prentice Hall)
   Chapters 7-24
3. *The Language of Medicine, 9th Edition* (Saunders)
   Chapter 21

Sample Questions

Each question below represents the kind of format and content, per the exam blue print, that an RMT candidate can expect to find on the RMT exam. *Note: These are sample questions only. They are questions that do not currently appear on the RMT exam. Though some may represent items retired from previous exam forms, not all items have been psychometrically analyzed, and AHDI cautions candidates against the presumption that these items alone may be diagnostic or indicative of candidate performance.* **(Answer key at end of chapter.)**

9. Which of the following medications is prescribed for a hypertensive patient?

   A. lisinopril
   B. tamoxifen
   C. dobutamine
   D. omeprazole

10. For what symptom would lorazepam be prescribed?

    A. cough
    B. anxiety
    C. nausea
    D. sinus pain

11. Which medication requires frequent monitoring of blood levels to ensure therapeutic dosing and is often discontinued several days prior to surgical procedures?

    A. Coumadin
    B. Lexapro
    C. insulin
    D. amoxicillin

12. A patient with osteoarthritis might be prescribed which medication?

    A. Lovenox
    B. Seroquel
    C. Celebrex
    D. Arimidex

Sample Questions Answer Key

1. C
2. B
3. B
4. C
5. B
6. A
7. C
8. B
9. A
10. B
11. A
12. C

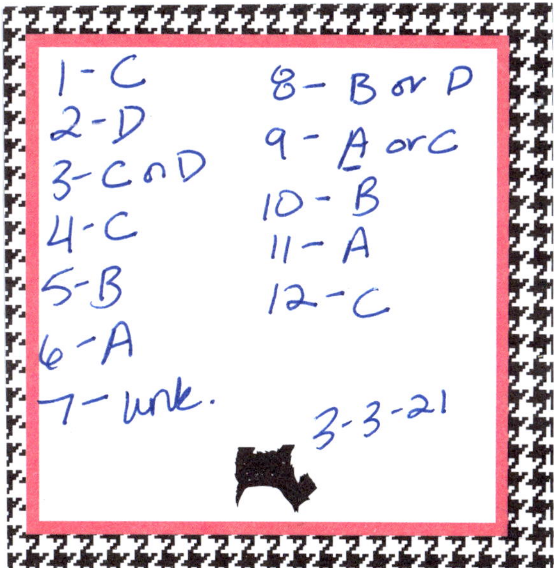

Anatomy, Physiology, and Disease

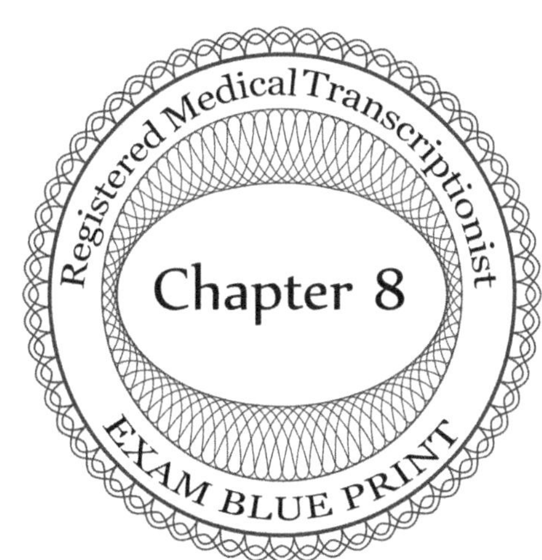

"Disease is a broad general concept, encompassing every imaginable impairment of normal bodily structure and function, and every imaginable threat to health and well-being...disease is a complex notion, including not only biological alterations of normal structure and function but also psychological, social, and economic factors."

– Human Diseases, 2nd Edition[1]

Chapter Overview

Anatomy (the structure of the body) and physiology (the processes of the body) together account for the most basic vocabulary of the language of medicine. All understanding of human disease is in turn based upon our understanding of the structure and function of the human body. These categories make up the most fundamental domain of the clinical medicine lexicon, a common language shared by physicians, nurses, technicians, health information professionals, and everyone concerned with patient care. A medical transcriptionist with a firm command of this domain will possess key knowledge that is the essential basis for the creation of healthcare documentation. As the healthcare documentation sector evolves, through the adoption of the electronic health record and into a suite of new roles involved in the creation, editing, and management of documentation, the medical transcriptionist who is thoroughly knowledgeable about anatomy, physiology, and disease will possess the flexibility to move into those new (yet to be delineated) roles.

---

[1] Dirckx, John H. MD. *Human Diseases.* Modesto: Health Professions Institute, 2003.

The body of knowledge for Level 1 medical transcriptionists therefore includes an understanding of:

- Basic terminology in common clinical specialties: *Alternative Medicine, Cardiovascular, Chiropractic, Dermatology, Endocrinology, Gastroenterology/Hepatology, General Surgery, Hematology/Oncology, Infectious Disease, Neurology, OB/Gyn, Ophthalmology, Orthopedics, Otorhinolaryngology, Pediatrics, Physical & Rehab Medicine, Psychiatry/Psychology, Pulmonary Medicine, and Urology.*
- The meaning of abbreviations commonly used in the above-listed areas of medicine.
- How to map the structures of the body, including organs and organ systems.
- The basic processes of human physiology.
- The ability to recognize the associations between symptoms and disease processes, and a basic knowledge of treatment courses for commonly occurring diseases.
- The use of classification systems in the description of diseases and pathologies.

There are **8 objectives**[2] on the RMT blue print that address concepts related to these domains and against which an RMT exam candidate will be evaluated. In this chapter, we will walk through each objective listed under *RMT Blue Print Section 2: Clinical Medicine* that relate to these domains.

Objective 2.17

Objective 2.17: *Given a clinical term, identify the correct definition, or given a definition, identify the correct clinical term.* ***See medical specialties above.***

---

[2] Objectives 2.19 and 2.29 on the RMT blue print is an audio objective that also relates to Anatomy, Physiology, and Disease. Look for blue print guidance on audio objectives in upcoming AHDI exam prep products.

Rationale

For the level 1 medical transcriptionist, the core knowledge set in anatomy and physiology centers upon the kinds of conditions, physiological processes, diseases, and pathologies most commonly occurring in areas of medicine such as those listed in this objective. Clearly, the transcription practitioner's vocabulary will grow with experience, but a solid grasp of basic terminology provides a firm foundation on which to build.

Recommendations for Focused Study

1. *The Book of Style for Medical Transcription, 3rd Edition*
   Section 4
2. *Principles of Anatomy and Physiology* (Wiley Publishing)
3. *Anatomy and Physiology Flash Cards Book* (Scientific Publishing)
4. *The Anatomy Coloring Book* (Benjamin Cummings, Publisher)

Sample Questions

Each question below represents the kind of format and content, per the exam blue print, that an RMT candidate can expect to find on the RMT exam. *Note: These are sample questions only. They are questions that do not currently appear on the RMT exam. Though some may represent items retired from previous exam forms, not all items have been psychometrically analyzed, and AHDI cautions candidates against the presumption that these items alone may be diagnostic or indicative of candidate performance.* **(Answer key at end of chapter.)**

1. Which is the correct definition of *menarche*?

   A. Increased frequency of menstrual cycles
   B. Absence of menstrual flow
   C. Permanent cessation of menses
   D. Onset of menstruation

2. **The patient presented with chest pain and diaphoresis.**

   What is the meaning of the underlined term in this excerpt?

   A. rapid heart beat

B. excessive sweating
C. extreme thirst
D. radiating pain

3. When the phrase *carcinoma in situ* is documented, what does *in situ* mean?

A. metastasized to secondary location
B. in its original location
C. no longer present on evaluation
D. evident to the naked eye

Objective 2.18

Objective 2.18: *Given a clinical abbreviation, identify the correct term, or given a term, identify the correct clinical abbreviation.* ***See medical specialties above.***

Rationale

The use of abbreviations is a common (some suggest *too* common) occurrence in clinical medicine. Used carefully, abbreviations can provide a means of short-hand communication of complex ideas and cumbersome verbiage. The medical transcriptionist can help ensure that abbreviations are used carefully, and that they are used appropriately in relevant medical context. Knowledge of any area of medical practice is not complete without a good basic grasp of the variety of abbreviations specific to that area, including the ability to judge whether an abbreviation is widely shared and understood, and of when (and how) to expand abbreviations for clarity.

Recommendations for Focused Study

1. *The Book of Style for Medical Transcription, 3rd Edition*
   Chapters 9, 13-24
2. *The Language of Medicine, 9th Edition* (Saunders)
   Chapters 5-22

3. *Stedman's Medical Terminology: Steps to Success in Medical Language* (Wolters Kluwer)
   Appendix D: Abbreviations

Sample Questions

Each question below represents the kind of format and content, per the exam blue print, that an RMT candidate can expect to find on the RMT exam. *Note: These are sample questions only. They are questions that do not currently appear on the RMT exam. Though some may represent items retired from previous exam forms, not all items have been psychometrically analyzed, and AHDI cautions candidates against the presumption that these items alone may be diagnostic or indicative of candidate performance.* **(Answer key at end of chapter.)**

4. What does the abbreviation CIS stand for?

   A. cardiac insufficiency syndrome
   B. carcinoma in stasis
   C. carcinoma in situ
   D. chronic ischemic syndrome

5. In psychiatry, what does the abbreviation GAF stand for?

   A. growth assessment factors
   B. general appearance of facies
   C. global assessment of functioning
   D. general assessment of function

6. **PAST MEDICAL HISTORY: Type 2 diabetes mellitus; status post left BKA.**

   What does the *A* in *BKA* refer to here?

   A. amputation
   B. assay
   C. augmentation
   D. attenuation

Objectives 2.20 and 2.21

Objective 2.20: *Given a graphic showing anatomy or systems, identify the anatomy or system involved.* ***See medical specialties above.***

Objective 2.21: *Given a position or location, identify the anatomical part of the human body.*

Rationale

A mental image of human anatomy and systems will often assist the medical transcriptionist in interpreting dictation and correctly transcribing healthcare documents. It will also reinforce the skill of the transcriptionist or editor as a monitor of documentation quality as part of the healthcare documentation team, and this mental image will allow the practitioner to make accurate judgments about when clarification from the document originator is required. Likewise, and for the same purposes, the transcriptionist needs a precise understanding of the spatial relationships in human anatomy: the location of organs relative to one another and to the planes of the body.

Recommendations for Focused Study

1. *The Book of Style for Medical Transcription, 3rd Edition*
   Section 4
2. *Principles of Anatomy and Physiology* (Wiley Publishing)
3. *Anatomy and Physiology Flash Cards Book* (Scientific Publishing)
4. *The Anatomy Coloring Book* (Benjamin Cummings, Publisher)

Sample Questions

Each question below represents the kind of format and content, per the exam blue print, that an RMT candidate can expect to find on the RMT exam. *Note: These are sample questions only. They are questions that do not currently appear on the RMT exam. Though some may represent items retired from previous exam forms, not all items have been psychometrically analyzed, and AHDI cautions candidates against the presumption that these items alone may be diagnostic or indicative of candidate performance.* **(Answer key at end of chapter.)**

7. What anatomic feature of the eye is indicated by the arrow in the picture at the right?

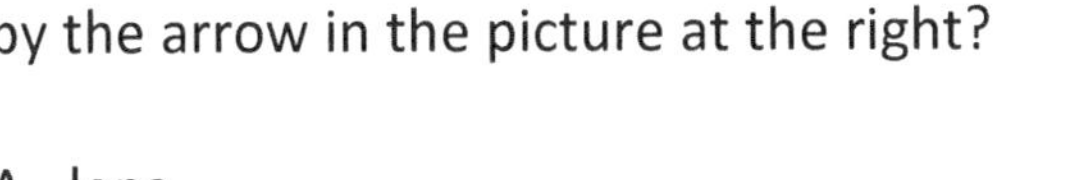

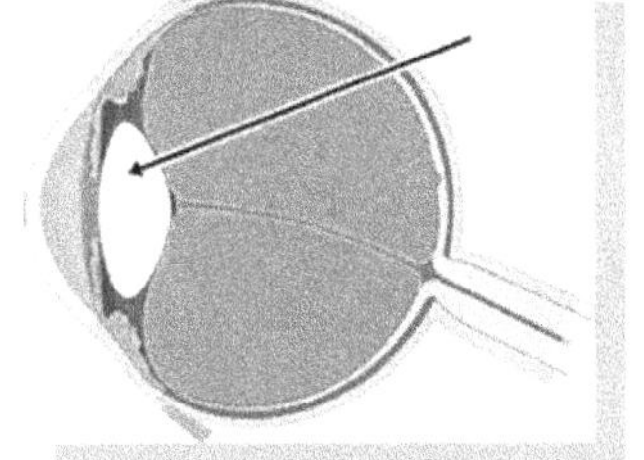

A. lens
B. retina
C. fovea
D. sclera

8. What part of the knee, also known as the kneecap, provides anterior protection for the knee joint?

A. fibula
B. anterior cruciate
C. meniscus
D. patella

9. In the picture to the right, what is the collective name of the bones in the shaded area?

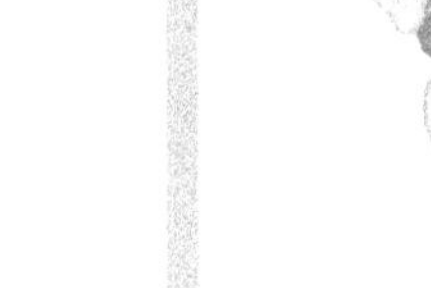

A. phalanges
B. carpals
C. metacarpals
D. metatarsals

10. Which teeth are located medial to the canines?

A. molars
B. second premolars
C. lateral incisors
D. first premolars

Objective 2.22

Objective 2.22: *Given a physiological process, identify steps or functions related to that process.*

Rationale

With cardiovascular conditions and diseases as a primary focus of 21st century medicine, the physiological processes relevant to the heart and the circulatory system are of particular importance to the beginning medical transcriptionist. Millions of individuals are under care for cardiovascular disorders, and new technologies have greatly expanded the diagnostic and treatment options in this specialty. In order to keep current with the ever-expanding trends in cardiovascular medicine, the transcriptionist must be very familiar with the basic physiologic processes involved in the closely intertwined systems of heart, lungs, and circulation.

Recommendations for Focused Study

1. *The Book of Style for Medical Transcription, 3rd Edition*
   Section 4
2. *Principles of Anatomy and Physiology* (Wiley Publishing)

Sample Questions

Each question below represents the kind of format and content, per the exam blue print, that an RMT candidate can expect to find on the RMT exam. *Note: These are sample questions only. They are questions that do not currently appear on the RMT exam. Though some may represent items retired from previous exam forms, not all items have been psychometrically analyzed, and AHDI cautions candidates against the presumption that these items alone may be diagnostic or indicative of candidate performance.* **(Answer key at end of chapter.)**

11. Which correctly describes the process of *systemic* circulation?

    A. veins deliver oxygenated blood to the heart
    B. arteries deliver deoxygenated blood to the heart
    C. veins deliver deoxygenated blood to the capillaries
    D. arteries deliver oxygenated blood to the capillaries

12. Which describes the correct order of blood flow through the heart?

A. left ventricle, right ventricle, lungs, left atrium, right atrium
B. lungs, left atrium, right atrium, right ventricle, left ventricle
C. right atrium, right ventricle, lungs, left atrium, left ventricle
D. right ventricle, right atrium, lungs, left ventricle, left atrium

13. Amylase and lipase serve what function in human physiology?

A. synthesizing proteins from amino acids
B. breaking down starches and fats to aid in digestion
C. generating an electrical impulse for cardiac contraction
D. regulating arterial blood pressure

Objectives 2.23 and 2.24

Objective 2.23: *Given a sign or symptom, identify the disease or syndrome.*

Objective 2.24: *Given a disease or syndrome, identify the treatment course.*

Rationale

Experienced medical transcriptionists sometimes find themselves mentally diagnosing a patient before the healthcare provider dictates the actual diagnoses. Because they are familiar with the symptom complexes associated with certain commonly occurring conditions, transcriptionists can, at times, anticipate what the document originator is going to conclude. This anticipation is no substitute, of course, for accurately transcribing what is actually dictated! But an understanding of associated symptoms and diagnoses can increase the transcriptionist's ability to correctly interpret dictation and to edit the document for accuracy and completeness. In the same way, knowledge of the usual treatment courses for frequently diagnosed conditions can also enhance both interpretation and assessment of dictated documentation, with a gain in patient safety and the quality of patient care delivery.

Recommendations for Focused Study

1. *The Book of Style for Medical Transcription, 3rd Edition*
   Section 4
2. *Principles of Anatomy and Physiology* (Wiley Publishing)
3. *Anatomy and Physiology Flash Cards Book* (Scientific Publishing)
4. *Stedman's Medical Terminology: Steps to Success in Medical Language* (Wolters Kluwer)
   Symptoms and Medical Conditions: Chapters 4-16
5. *Human Diseases, 2nd Edition* (Health Professions Institute)
   Chapters 1-20
6. *The Language of Medicine, 9th Edition* (Saunders)
   Abnormal Conditions: Chapters 5-19
7. *Medical Transcription Fundaments: Where Success Takes Root, 2nd Edition* (Wolters Kluwer)
   Common Diseases and Treatments: Chapters 9-21

Sample Questions

Each question below represents the kind of format and content, per the exam blue print, that an RMT candidate can expect to find on the RMT exam. *Note: These are sample questions only. They are questions that do not currently appear on the RMT exam. Though some may represent items retired from previous exam forms, not all items have been psychometrically analyzed, and AHDI cautions candidates against the presumption that these items alone may be diagnostic or indicative of candidate performance.* **(Answer key at end of chapter.)**

14. Extreme thirst, excess urination, and unexplained weight loss may indicate the presence of what disease?

    A. Addison disease
    B. diabetes mellitus
    C. pulmonary edema
    D. hypothyroidism

15. What condition may present with symptoms of shortness of breath, swelling of ankles and feet, abdominal swelling, and persistent cough with phlegm production?

   A. acute bronchitis
   B. hypoparathyroidism
   C. hyperparathyroidism
   D. congestive heart failure

16. Which is an interventional procedure for eradicating kidney stones?

   A. ESWL
   B. CABG
   C. ORIF
   D. EGD

17. An endarterectomy procedure would be performed to treat which cardiovascular condition?

   A. coronary artery disease
   B. carotid artery disease
   C. myocardial infarction
   D. mitral valve prolapse

Objective 2.28

Objective 2.28: *Given a classification system, identify the expressed score or grade, or given a classification system result, identify the disease or affected anatomical part.*

Rationale

As elsewhere in the science and practice of medicine, classification systems form an integral part of recording and communicating about diseases and conditions. It is vitally important that these classification systems be correctly transcribed and that the classificatory systems be used appropriately; the knowledgeable medical transcriptionist contributes to both of these goals.

Recommendations for Focused Study

The Book of Style for Medical Transcription, 3rd Edition

Section 14.3; Section 24.2; Section 17.1.3; Section 19.1.4; Section 19.2.3; Section 16.2.2; Section 20.3; Section 18.1.5; Section 18.2.4; Section 22.2; Section 23.3

Sample Questions

Each question below represents the kind of format and content, per the exam blue print, that an RMT candidate can expect to find on the RMT exam. *Note: These are sample questions only. They are questions that do not currently appear on the RMT exam. Though some may represent items retired from previous exam forms, not all items have been psychometrically analyzed, and AHDI cautions candidates against the presumption that these items alone may be diagnostic or indicative of candidate performance.* **(Answer key at end of chapter.)**

18. A condition classified as NYHA I is describing what condition?

    A. kidney failure
    B. cardiac failure
    C. coronary artery disease
    D. chronic obstructive lung disease

19. A LeFort II fracture would be found in what part of the body?

    A. skull
    B. spine
    C. pelvis
    D. thorax

20. Which refers to a classification system used to score bladder carcinoma?

    A. Clark
    B. FAB
    C. Jewett
    D. Breslow

Sample Questions Answer Key

1. D
2. B
3. B
4. C
5. C
6. A
7. A
8. D
9. B
10. C
11. D
12. C
13. B
14. B
15. D
16. A
17. B
18. B
19. A
20. C

Section 3

Health Information Technology

"I recently changed jobs and had to submit resumes to prospective employers. Being a CMT automatically offered me the opportunity to apply for jobs and test without any "pre-screening" of my skill sets. After being hired, I was immediately offered a position in Quality Assurance even before I had learned the accounts! This was based on my credential and, of course, my experience. But without the credential, I would not have been offered the opportunity to move from an MLS position to a QA job within the first 2 weeks of my employment with a new company. My credentials have consistently opened doors of opportunity for me." – Carrie Boatman, CMT, AHDI-F

Computer Fundamentals

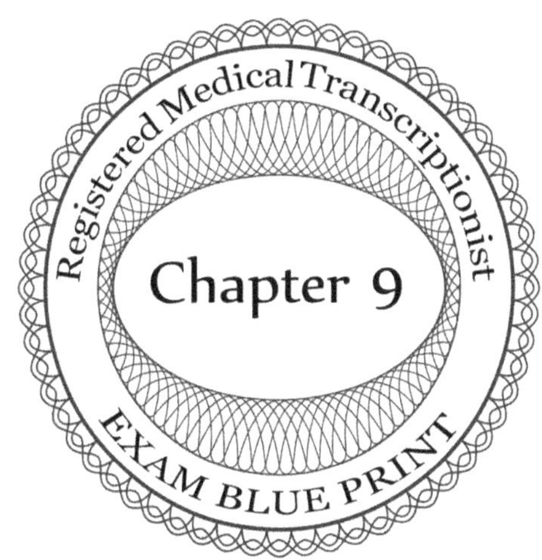

"Using your computer efficiently and taking advantage of its power and resources means you work smarter, not harder. A higher level of proficiency with computers and electronic resources also increases the accuracy of your documents and contributes to patient safety and risk management."

– **Technology for the Medical Transcriptionist**[1]

Chapter Overview

Since the late 1970s, computers have been used by medical transcriptionists in the creation of healthcare records. Always closely involved in the evolution of health information technology, transcriptionists have seen the transition from typewriters and paper records into mainframe and personal computers, and into the digital transformation of record-keeping and information exchange. The growing adoption of a completely electronic health record is the most recent, and arguably the most far-reaching, of these ongoing changes. To function in this environment, the medical transcription practitioner cannot merely be a passive user of computer technology. To be a fully active member of the healthcare documentation team, the practitioner must speak the language of information technology and have the ability to communicate well with the technologists who enable us to work efficiently and effectively for patient care and safety.

The body of knowledge for medical transcriptionists therefore includes an understanding of:

---

[1] Bryan, Laura MT (ASCP), CMT, AHDI-F. *Technology for the Medical Transcriptionist.* Baltimore: Wolters Kluwer, 2010.

- The correct expansions for abbreviations commonly used in computer terminology.
- The ability to correctly define computer technology terms.

There are **2 objectives** on the RMT blue print that address concepts related to these domains and against which an RMT exam candidate will be evaluated. In this chapter, we will walk through each objective listed under *RMT Blue Print Section 3: Health Information Technology* that relate to these domains.

Objectives 3.1 and 3.2

Objective 3.1: *Given the abbreviation of a computer term, identify the correct expanded form.*

Objective 3.2: *Given a computer technology term, identify the correct definition, or given a definition, identify the correct computer technology term.*

Rationale

Computer technology communication very frequently employs the shorthand of abbreviations. In fact, many computer technology terms are never expanded in day-to-day use. Though electronic systems will change, certain terms in their shorthand versions will form a body of basic knowledge, and the practitioner who understands these basics will have the flexibility to continue to adapt to the evolving technological environment. Likewise, the medical transcriptionist must understand the basics of computer operation in order to facilitate accurate communication with information technology subject matter experts; knowing which keys to hit is not enough! Basic terminology describing how computers work must be part of the transcriptionist's vocabulary.

Recommendations for Focused Study

Technology for the Medical Transcriptionist (Wolters Kluwer)
Chapters 1-14

Sample Questions

Each question below represents the kind of format and content, per the exam blue print, that an RMT candidate can expect to find on the RMT exam. *Note: These are sample questions only. They are questions that* *<u>do not</u>* *currently appear on the RMT exam. Though some may represent items retired from previous exam forms, not all items have been psychometrically analyzed, and AHDI cautions candidates against the presumption that these items alone may be diagnostic or indicative of candidate performance.* **(Answer key at end of chapter.)**

1. What is the meaning of XML?

   A. extensible markup language
   B. electronic markup language
   C. electronic medical language
   D. extensible medical language

2. Which serves as the "brain" of the computer?

   A. motherboard
   B. CPU
   C. USB
   D. hard drive

3. Processor speed is measured in which units?

   A. hertz
   B. bits
   C. bytes
   D. pixels

4. Which term is used to refer to the process of copying data from a CD to a computer hard drive?

   A. burn
   B. upload

C. rip
D. transfer

5. What does the *I* in *GUI* refer to?

A. information
B. interface
C. index
D. indicator

6. What function does the F5 key perform in Windows?

A. Refreshes the current window
B. Opens Windows Help
C. Moves up one folder level
D. Activates the menu bar

7. Holding down the CTRL button while scrolling the mouse wheel will perform what action in most Microsoft applications?

A. Minimize
B. Maximize
C. Select text
D. Zoom

8. Which refers to a collaborative website that can be directly edited by anyone with access to it?

A. wiki
B. RSS
C. blog
D. ISP

Sample Questions Answer Key

1. A
2. B
3. A
4. C
5. B
6. A
7. D
8. A

Industry Terms and Technologies

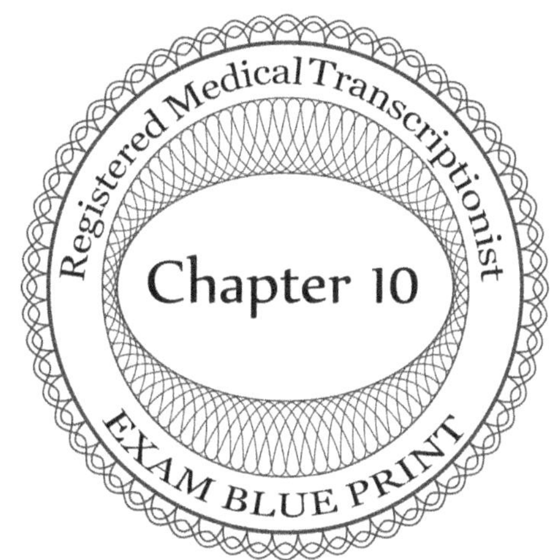

"Unfortunately, the transcription industry uses a broad range of equipment and technologies to record, distribute, and transcribe reports, and there is very little standardization of methods. Technology is a dynamic topic and is changing swiftly."

– **Technology for the Medical Transcriptionist**[1]

Chapter Overview

Beyond the basics of computer technology, the medical transcriptionist is going to encounter language specific to technological applications in healthcare documentation. These close encounters with a specialized technical vocabulary will continue throughout the practitioner's career, and the language itself will evolve as all technical languages do. The medical transcriptionist entering the profession must be comfortable with basic health information technology terminology, and this will be the foundation on which the continued process of career-long learning will be built.

The body of knowledge for Level 1 medical transcriptionists therefore includes an understanding of:

- The correct expansions for abbreviations commonly used in health information terminology.
- The ability to correctly define health information technology terms.

---

[1] Bryan, Laura MT (ASCP), CMT, AHDI-F. *Technology for the Medical Transcriptionist.* Baltimore: Wolters Kluwer, 2010.

- The technologies involved in the secure and reliable exchange of health information.

There are **3 objectives** on the RMT blue print that address concepts related to these domains and against which an RMT exam candidate will be evaluated. In this chapter, we will walk through each objective listed under *RMT Blue Print Section 3: Health Information Technology* that relate to these domains.

Objectives 3.3 and 3.4

Objective 3.3: *Given the abbreviation of a healthcare documentation technology term, identify the correct expanded form.*

Objective 3.4: *Given a healthcare documentation technology term, identify the correct definition, or given a definition, identify the correct healthcare documentation technology term.*

Rationale

Like other areas of health care, health information technology employs many abbreviations. In fact, the use of abbreviations may be even more central to communication in the technological realm than it is in other areas; as with computer technology language, many information technology abbreviations (which sometimes express very complex ideas) are almost never expanded. However, the medical transcriptionist or editor must know what these abbreviations mean in order to ensure correct usage. Again, as in other areas of health care, abbreviations, though useful, can pose risks of miscommunication. In general, with the adoption of the electronic health record across the United States (and internationally), terms used to talk about electronic documentation in clinical practice will become more and more essential to the medical transcriptionist's vocabulary. The successful level 1 practitioner will enter the field with a command of the basics of the language of healthcare information technology. This basic vocabulary will furnish the building blocks for continued flexibility and learning as health information technology evolves into the future.

Recommendations for Focused Study

1. *The Book of Style for Medical Transcription, 3rd Edition*
   Chapters 25-28; Appendix E
2. *Technology for the Medical Transcriptionist* (Wolters Kluwer)
   Chapter 15
3. *EHR Readiness Tool Kit: EHR & Technology Abbreviations & Acronyms*
   (www.ahdionline.org)

Sample Questions

Each question below represents the kind of format and content, per the exam blue print, that an RMT candidate can expect to find on the RMT exam. *Note: These are sample questions only. They are questions that do not currently appear on the RMT exam. Though some may represent items retired from previous exam forms, not all items have been psychometrically analyzed, and AHDI cautions candidates against the presumption that these items alone may be diagnostic or indicative of candidate performance.* **(Answer key at end of chapter.)**

1. What is the correct expansion of CPOE?

   A. clinical practice order entry
   B. computerized physician order entry
   C. clinical and procedural operations entry
   D. clinic procedures and operations entities

2. In terms of healthcare technology, what does the abbreviation CDS stand for?

   A. clinical data stream
   B. clinical decision support
   C. clinical decision standards
   D. clinical documentation of standards

3. Which refers to the integration of transcribed reports into EHR templates?

   A. direct record templating
   B. direct reentry transcription

C. discrete records templating
D. discrete reportable transcription

4. Which technology is used to manage the storage, access, and rapid retrieval of radiographic images?

A. VPN
B. PACS
C. ISDN
D. BC-MAR

5. Which organization sets international standards for materials, products, systems, and services?

A. Joint Commission
B. AHIMA
C. ASTM
D. HL7

Objective 3.5

Objective 3.5: *Given a term or abbreviation related to transcription technology or data exchange, identify the correct definition, or given a definition related to transcription technology or data exchange, identify the term or abbreviation.*

Rationale

The growth of the electronic health record has in turn caused some major changes in the technology that the practicing medical transcriptionist uses daily. New tools have been, and continue to be, developed for record creation by transcriptionists and for delivery of records to healthcare providers, researchers, government agencies, and insurance companies. Each of these new systems carries with it a unique lexicon. These terms, describing medical transcription practice in an electronic world, must be part of the vocabulary of transcriptionists from the beginning of their careers. In addition, the exchange of health information reliably and safely is an absolute essential element in the expanding electronic health record system. In fact, one of the goals for the development of a national electronic records system in the United States is to facilitate care of patients across providers who might be physically separated from one another. In addition, accurately transmitted data about patient care will facilitate both medical research and reimbursement. As members of the healthcare information team, medical transcriptionists need an understanding of the basic terms and principles of data exchange systems.

Recommendations for Focused Study

1. *The Book of Style for Medical Transcription, 3rd Edition*
   Chapters 25-28; Appendix E
2. *Technology for the Medical Transcriptionist* (Wolters Kluwer)
   Chapter 15
3. *EHR Readiness Tool Kit: EHR & Technology Abbreviations & Acronyms*
   (www.ahdionline.org)

Sample Questions

Each question below represents the kind of format and content, per the exam blue print, that an RMT candidate can expect to find on the RMT exam. *Note: These are sample questions only. They are questions that do not currently appear on the RMT exam. Though some may represent items retired from previous exam forms, not all items have been psychometrically analyzed, and AHDI cautions candidates against the presumption that these items alone may be diagnostic or indicative of candidate performance.* **(Answer key at end of chapter.)**

6. Which is a common file format used in transcription for digital audio?

   A. .doc
   B. .wmv
   C. .wav
   D. .wps

7. What does the *A* stand for in *TASP*?

   A. application
   B. area
   C. aggregate
   D. acquisition

8. Which refers to individual pieces of information that can be uniquely classified?

   A. concrete
   B. discrete
   C. complete
   D. repeat

9. With which technology would a physician dictate a narrative and then edit the draft without the use of a transcriptionist?

   A. BESR
   B. TASP
   C. FESR
   D. CPOE

10. Which organization was established by the federal government to certify products that meet or exceed standards for EHR usability and interoperability?

   A. HIMSS
   B. ASTM
   C. HITSP
   D. CCHIT

Sample Questions Answer Key

1. B
2. B
3. D
4. B
5. C
6. C
7. A
8. B
9. C
10. D

Section 4

Cognitive Assessment

"I have seen our profession change many times in the last 30 years but the one thing that never changes is this, you have to know what you are doing and you have to have some way to show that you know this. Being certified is the best possible way to do this. Staying certified is the best possible way to stay current with your profession and understand the changes that are constantly occurring. I'm very proud of what I do and being certified is the best way to project that." – Helga H. Friedland, CMT

RMT Practice Test

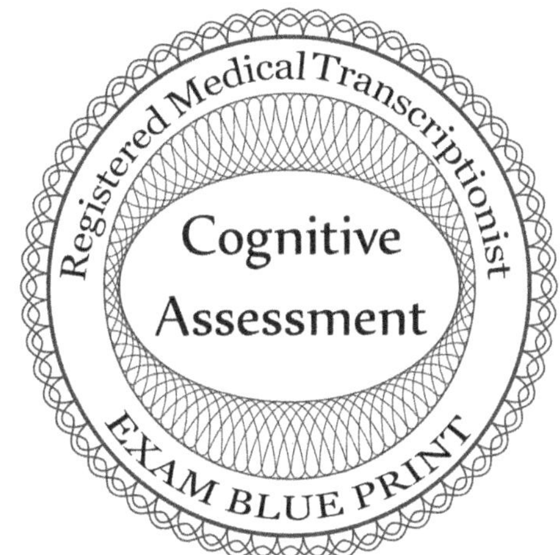

"Practice does not make perfect. Perfect practice makes perfect."

– Vince Lombardi

Instructions

The RMT exam houses 91 cognitive assessment (multiple-choice) questions and 39 audio items. Below you will find a 91-question practice test designed to parallel the weight and balance of objectives on the RMT exam itself. None of the questions below are taken from the exam, but they represent potential content domains under the blue print to which you have now been oriented by this text. They should give you an overall impression of exam scope and format, though AHDI cautions candidates against the presumption that these items alone may be diagnostic or indicative of exam performance. To assist you with identifying weaknesses under specific objectives, the questions here follow the order of the exam blue print, but keep in mind that items on the RMT exam are *randomized* and will not be identified by objective or competency. **(Answer key on page 123.)**

1. **Livor is posterior and blanching.**

   In what report type would this statement be found?

   A. Pathology report
   B. Autopsy
   C. Operative report
   D. Emergency department report

2. **The patient is gravida 2, para 2.**

Under which report heading would this information be transcribed?

A. DISPOSITION
B. PHYSICAL EXAMINATION
C. LABORATORY RESULTS
D. PAST MEDICAL HISTORY

3. **D: 12/21/11, 0800**
T: 12/22/11, 0300

What is the primary purpose for the notation above in a clinical report?

A. Identify turn-around time
B. Establish an audit trail
C. Track reimbursement
D. Reflect the date of treatment

4. Which sentence requires editing by the transcriptionist?

A. The patient is unable to accept the diagnosis.
B. This patient is averse to taking any medications.
C. The patient underwent drainage of ascitic fluid from his abdomen.
D. In his history, the patient eluded to previous substance abuse.

5. **DICTATED: We used a mets to open the hernia sac.**

How should this be transcribed?

A. We used Metzenbaum scissors to open the hernia sac.
B. We used a Metzenbaum scissor to open the hernia sac.
C. We used a Metz scissor to open the hernia sac.
D. We used Metz scissors to open the hernia sac.

6. Demographic information provided by your ADT data indicates the patient's name is Michael Jones. The physician dictates: *This 50-year-old female patient presents with an inguinal hernia.* In terms of transcription best practices, what do you do?

A. Remove the word *female.*
B. Flag the report for clarification.
C. Change the dictated word *female* to *male.*
D. Insert *Michael Jones* after the word *patient.*

7. In terms of health record privacy, what does the abbreviation OCR stand for?

A. Office of Civil Rights
B. Office for Coordination of Records
C. Official Clearance for Release
D. Official Clarification of Record

8. According to HIPAA privacy regulations, which represents an inappropriate disclosure of PHI?

A. A hospital faxes a list of a patient's medications to a consulting physician's office without prior authorization from the patient.
B. A physician drops into another physician's office and discusses a patient's treatment course.
C. After transcribing a report about her own cousin, an MT immediately sends another family member an email describing the physician's findings.
D. An MTSO performs data aggregation services on behalf of a covered entity, in accordance with a business associate agreement.

9. Which MT is considered a business associate by HIPAA (HITECH) definition?

A. An MT who contracts from home for a private practice in his/her local community.
B. An MT who is an employee working remotely for a small clinic in another community.
C. An MT transcribing as an employee for a medical transcription service provider.
D. An MT who is an employee working remotely for an acute-care hospital.

10. What is recommended by the Book of Style for electronic system security?

A. The computer used for medical transcription should be located in a locked room.
B. Post a sign stating "authorized personnel only" on the home office.
C. Create an "invisible drive" for storage of PHI so the rest of the family can safely use the computer.
D. Change passwords once a year.

11. According to the Book of Style, when is it necessary to encrypt PHI?

A. When a file containing PHI is attached to an email.
B. When PHI is being discussed on a mobile phone.
C. When faxing PHI to a consulting practice.
D. When PHI is being provided to the patient after discharge.

12. Which authentication practice is considered dangerous by the Joint Commission?

A. Handwritten signature
B. Electronic initialing
C. Third-party signature
D. Handwritten initials

13. Which sentence demonstrates correct pronoun usage?

A. For him and I, there's only one therapy available.
B. The physician expects you and me to follow his instructions.
C. It's up to you and I to perform the exercises correctly.
D. Me and him are expected to come to therapy together.

14. Which sentence is correct?

A. Chemotherapy does not always affect a cure.
B. Chemotherapy does not always effect a cure.
C. The affect of chemotherapy is sometimes dramatic.
D. In some cases, chemotherapy is affective.

15. Which sentence is correctly punctuated?

A. The infant's birth weight was 9 pounds, 2 ounces.
B. Today the infant is 2 months 5 days old.
C. The infant is being given: Tylenol Elixir and home aerosol.
D. The child was having seizures every morning, at night, no seizures.

16. Which is transcribed correctly?

A. She was given a new appointment with the Anesthesiologist.
B. We were unable to reach the child's Mother.
C. Exam revealed a cushingoid appearance.
D. We sent the patient to the Emergency Room.

17. Which sentence contains a correctly expressed Latin term?

A. One criteria for diagnosis is the presence of a rash.
B. This phenomena is rarely seen in the elderly.
C. She has suffered several sickle cell crises.
D. The adnexa is normal.

18. Which phrase shows the correct expression of a possessive?

A. several witness' descriptions of the accident
B. several witnesses description of the accident
C. several witness's description of the accident
D. several witnesses' description of the accident

19. Which is the correct abbreviation for the instruction "nothing by mouth"?

A. a.c.
B. n.r.
C. n.p.r.
D. n.p.o

20. Which expression is correctly transcribed?

A. OPERATIVE PROCEDURES
   Bilateral myringotomy tube placement and tonsillectomy and adenoidectomy.
B. OPERATIVE PROCEDURES
   BMT with tonsillectomy and adenoidectomy.
C. OPERATIVE PROCEDURES
   Bilateral myringotomy tube placement, T&A
D. OPERATIVE PROCEDURES
   BMT, T&A.

21. Which abbreviation appears on the Joint Commission list of dangerous abbreviations?

A. I.U.
B. n.r.
C. mEq
D. DNR

22. Which sentence contains a correct expression of numbers?

A. There was a 5 cm laceration of the forearm.
B. There was a 5-cm laceration of the forearm.
C. There was a 5-in laceration of the forearm.
D. There was a 5 inch laceration of the forearm.

23. **Birth weight was _______.**

What is the correct form of numerical value in the above sentence?

A. 6 lbs 2 oz
B. 6-lb 2-oz
C. 6 pounds, 2 ounces
D. 6 pounds 2 ounces

24. **The patient was admitted at twenty thirty hours.**

What is the correct transcription of the above dictation?

A. The patient was admitted at 20-30 hours.
B. The patient was admitted at 2030 hours.
C. The patient was admitted at 8:30 a.m.
D. The patient was admitted at 20:30 p.m.

25. For which of the following are arabic numerals required?

A. histologic grades
B. cancer stages
C. Pap test classes
D. Dukes classification

26. Which proportion is correctly expressed?

A. Patient was instructed to exercise 3 times/week.
B. She reports taking 81 mg of aspirin/day.
C. IV was running at 5 mcg/min.
D. Add 3/1 glucose to water.

27. Which sentence represents the correct clinical application of a unit of measure?

A. The laceration measured 10 mmHg.
B. The area of laceration was 3 m/s.
C. The pressure was 10 Hz.
D. The PR interval was 155 msec.

28. **The pattern shows a frequency of about 4 ___.**

What is the correct unit of measure for the above blank?

A. Hz
B. mmol
C. mmHg
D. mCi

29. The word meaning "to draw toward the median line" is formed using what prefix?

A. ad-
B. ab-
C. trans-
D. en-

30. What is the combining form used for a term meaning red blood cells or corpuscles?

A. erythro-
B. arterio-
C. vascul-
D. cysto-

31. What is the focus of the medical specialty bariatrics?

A. old-age-related conditions
B. diseases of the bile ducts
C. obesity-related conditions
D. sports-related injuries

32. Which sentence correctly describes the position of the sclera in the globe of the eye?

A. It is the deepest layer.
B. It is the most superficial layer.
C. It is found throughout all layers.
D. It is the middle pigmented layer.

33. Which condition is found in scleroderma?

A. colorblindness
B. arteriosclerosis
C. softening of the skin
D. thickening of the skin

34. **A portion of the ilium was removed for use in grafting**

The graft was removed from which anatomical location?

A. bony pelvis
B. large intestine
C. small intestine
D. spinal vertebrae

35. Which sentence reflects the correct use of the term *xerosis*?

A. The patient's plantar surfaces showed severe xerosis.
B. A CT scan suggested hepatic xerosis.
C. Patients with xerosis must avoid alcohol.
D. The ovaries showed xerosis cystadenoma.

36. Which bone forms a part of the axial skeleton?

A. pubis
B. capitate
C. humerus
D. sphenoid

37. Where is an inguinal hernia located?

A. groin
B. spinal cord
C. upper abdomen
D. brain

38. Which value would be included in a complete blood count?

A. ANA
B. TSH
C. CD4
D. MCHC

39. Which laboratory test includes a value for specific gravity?

A. urinalysis
B. coagulation study
C. differential
D. arterial blood gas

40. Which value falls within the normal range for a white blood count?

A. 1000
B. 20,000
C. 8000
D. 30,000

41. For what liver function test would a value of 3 U/L would be normal?

A. ALT
B. AST
C. alkaline phosphatase
D. total bilirubin

42. Which study is used to study the structure and function of joints?

A. DXA scan
B. angiogram
C. arthrography
D. myelography

43. What kind of diagnostic imaging study assists in evaluation of colonic polyps?

A. scintigraphy
B. barium enema
C. iodine uptake
D. V/Q scan

44. What kind of imaging study can be enhanced using Doppler measurements?

A. sonography
B. scintigraphy

C. DEXA
D. plain x-ray

45. A perfusion mismatch might be found on what kind of study?

A. plain x-ray
B. V/Q scan
C. PET scan
D. MRI

46. What value is included in an electrolyte panel?

A. troponin
B. potassium
C. testosterone
D. urea nitrogen

47. What does the anion gap test assess?

A. oxygen saturation
B. ferritin level
C. ammonia level
D. metabolic acidosis

48. How can the drug fentanyl be administered?

A. by injection
B. either by injection or orally
C. by injection, orally, or transdermally
D. by injection, orally, transdermally, or by inhalation

49. Which drug is only administered intramuscularly or intravenously?

A. fentanyl
B. morphine
C. ketamine
D. diazepam

50. This class of drugs acts on the sympathetic nervous system to relieve stress on the heart.

A. antitussives
B. beta blockers
C. cephalosporins
D. benzodiazepines

51. What do the drugs halothane, isoflurane, and desflurane have in common?

A. They are all administered intramuscularly.
B. They are all antibiotics.
C. They are all inhalational anesthetics.
D. They are all administered per rectum.

52. Which of the following is a brand name for ketoconazole?

A. Neoral
B. Nitropress
C. Nasarel
D. Nizoral

53. What is the generic form of the drug Zantac?

A. zidovudine
B. ranitidine
C. zolpidem
D. reserpine

54. The suffix *–iazide* is common to which classification of drugs?

A. antidepressants
B. diuretics
C. beta blockers
D. decongestants

55. Which of the following is an anticonvulsant?

A. Depakene
B. Tobrex
C. Tofranil
D. Depo-Provera

56. For which of the following is Phenergan prescribed?

A. gastric ulcers
B. onychomycosis
C. allergic rhinitis
D. vaginitis

57. What drug is used to induce labor?

A. amoxicillin
B. oxytocin
C. terbutaline
D. tetracycline

58. What is the correct definition of a Colles fracture?

A. fracture of the lower end of the radius with displacement of the distal fragment
B. fracture of the navicular bone
C. fracture of the facial bones with a horizontal fracture at the base of the maxilla
D. fracture of the ulna with dislocation of the radial head

59. Which refers to narrowing of the opening of the prepuce, which prevents it from being drawn back over the glans?

A. phlebitis
B. phimosis
C. philomimesia
D. phlegmon

60. In pulmonary medicine, what does the abbreviation IPP stand for?

A. intrapulmonary pressure
B. intermittent positive pressure
C. interpulmonary pressure
D. intermediate pulmonary pressure

61. Which abbreviation represents a disorder in which stomach contents come back up from the stomach into the esophagus?

A. GIRD
B. GERD
C. GITS
D. GEST

62. The organ pictured to the right is part of which body system?

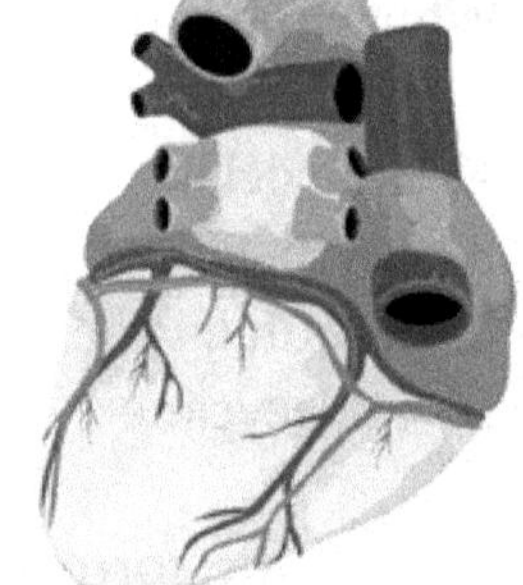

A. gastrointestinal
B. musculoskeletal
C. respiratory
D. cardiovascular

63. What is the name given to the lower posterior part of the hip bone, consisting of a body and a ramus?

A. ischium
B. ala
C. coccyx
D. sacrum

64. What medical specialty is concerned with the anatomical area represented by this picture?

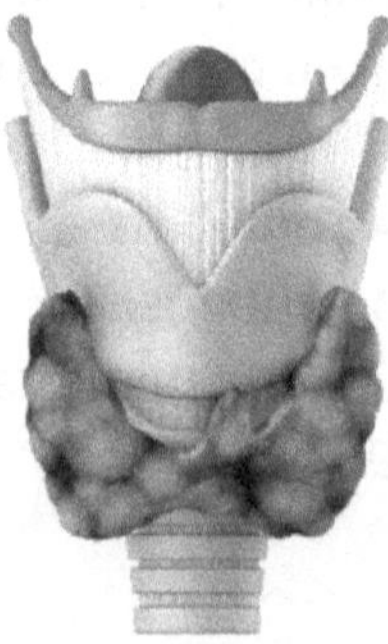

A. obstetrics-gynecology
B. orthopedics
C. ENT
D. urology

65. What arteries begin at the inguinal ligament and end just above the knee?

A. tibial
B. femoral
C. epigastric
D. inferior mesenteric

66. Which phrase correctly describes the path of the electrical impulse in a heartbeat?

A. From ventricles to atrioventricular node, then to sinoatrial node.
B. From the ventricles to the sinoatrial node, then to the atrioventricular node.
C. From the atrioventricular node to the sinoatrial node, then to the ventricles.
D. From the sinoatrial node to the atrioventricular node, then to the ventricles.

67. During cardiac systole, what occurs?

A. The left ventricle empties into the aorta.
B. The right ventricle empties into the aorta.
C. The left ventricle empties into the pulmonary artery.
D. The ventricles relax and accept blood from the atria.

68. Hyperpigmentation of the skin, low blood pressure, and salt craving may be signs of what condition?

A. diabetes insipidus
B. Crohn disease
C. Addison disease
D. diabetes mellitus

69. What condition may be indicated by a rash in a bull's-eye pattern accompanied by flu-like symptoms and, if untreated, joint pains?

A. osteomyelitis
B. lichen planus
C. amyotrophic lateral sclerosis
D. Lyme disease

70. What kind of tube might be placed to treat a patient with frequently recurring acute otitis media?

A. PEG tube
B. corneal tube
C. post-pyloric tube
D. tympanostomy tube

71. Which is a treatment course for lupus erythematosus?

A. NSAIDs, Plaquenil, and sun avoidance
B. penicillin, NSAIDs, and antacids
C. oxygen, corticosteroids, and blood transfusions
D. caloric restriction, exercise, and Plaquenil

72. Which is a correct expression in the Tanner classification system?

A. level III
B. stage 1
C. grade 0
D. axis B

73. The invasion level of primary malignant melanoma is classified using what system?

A. Clark
B. Mohs
C. Rule of Nines
D. G-CSFs

74. Which of the following correctly expands the term FTP?

A. finalized transfer protocol
B. formal transfer protocol
C. file transfer protocol
D. file termination protocol

75. Which expansion is correct for CPU?

A. central portal unit
B. computer portal unit
C. central processing unit
D. computer processor unit

76. What does RAM stand for?

A. randomly accessed memory
B. rapidly accessible memory
C. random access memory
D. rapid access memory

77. Which acronym stands for a business that hosts and manages software services for customers over a network?

A. ICD
B. ASP
C. CPT
D. RSS

78. What is the correct definition of HTML?

A. An electronic network
B. A syntax-defining format in a web page
C. A format for the display of medical information
D. A hybrid system combining templates and narrative text

79. What functionality allows a computer user to click and drag objects with a mouse instead of entering text commands?

A. GIS
B. GNU
C. GPS
D. GUI

80. In terms of healthcare documentation, what does the abbreviation HIE stand for?

A. hardware interface effectiveness
B. health insurance environment
C. health information exchange
D. health information entries

81. What is the correct expansion of the abbreviation CDR?

A. clinical data record
B. clinical data repository
C. clinical document reports
D. clinical documentation repository

82. Which is the correct expanded form of OCR?

A. optically certified records
B. online creation of records
C. optical character recognition
D. overall character recognition

83. What do the letters HL stand for in the term HL7?

A. Health Level
B. Healthcare Level
C. Host Location
D. Host Level

84. What is an enterprise-wide master patient index?

A. Information for certain subsets of patients.
B. All information available for a particular patient.
C. Information from overlapping patient populations.
D. Information available for certain applications such as clinical decision making.

85. Document imaging and clinical messaging are examples of what?

A. critical paths
B. bridge technologies
C. closed EHR systems
D. comprehensive use of an EHR

86. What is Clinical Document Architecture?

A. an electronic blue print for designing delivery of care
B. a protocol setting standards for documents to conform with ICD-9
C. an electronic exchange model developed by HL7 for healthcare documents
D. a plan for transitioning clinical documentation from paper to electronic media

87. What is the name of the US government agency tasked with guiding the nationwide implementation of health information technology?

A. Office of the National Coordinator
B. Health Information Exchange
C. Regional Extension Center
D. Office of Civil Rights

88. Which correctly describes front-end editing of documents created by speech recognition technology?

A. The document is edited by a medical transcriptionist, who then returns it to the originator for authentication and finalizing.

B. The document is edited by a medical transcriptionist, who then authenticates and finalizes it.
C. The document is edited by the originator, who then authenticates and finalizes it.
D. The document is edited by an individual of the originator's choice; that individual then authenticates and finalizes it.

89. What is an organization that promotes the exchange of healthcare data within a national network?

A. Office of Civil Rights
B. Clinical Context Object Workgroup
C. Regional Health Information Organization
D. Health Plan Employer Information Data Set

90. What is an example of structured data?

A. A history and physical transcribed as a Microsoft Word document
B. A plain x-ray of the lungs
C. A handwritten progress note scanned into a computer
D. A set of patient demographics

91. What is SNOMED?

A. A clinical reference terminology
B. A set of standards for objective data mining
C. A group of codes for reimbursement
D. A set of groups of synonyms

RMT Practice Test Answer Key

1. B
2. D
3. B
4. D
5. A
6. B
7. A
8. C
9. A
10. A
11. A
12. C
13. B
14. B
15. B
16. C
17. C
18. D
19. D
20. A
21. A
22. A
23. D
24. B
25. A
26. C
27. D
28. A
29. A
30. A
31. C
32. B
33. D
34. A
35. A
36. D
37. A
38. D
39. A
40. C

41. B
42. C
43. B
44. A
45. B
46. B
47. D
48. C
49. C
50. B
51. C
52. D
53. B
54. B
55. A
56. C
57. B
58. A
59. B
60. B
61. B
62. D
63. A
64. C
65. B
66. D
67. A
68. C
69. D
70. D
71. A
72. B
73. A
74. C
75. C
76. C
77. B
78. B
79. D
80. C
81. B
82. C
83. A
84. C

85. B
86. C
87. A
88. C
89. C
90. D
91. A

Appendices

Appendix A - RMT Recommended Resources List

The following is a resource list for all the texts cited in this book that are recommended for exam preparation and focused study.

Ethical Best Practices: Resource Guide for Healthcare Documentation Specialists
Publisher: Association for Healthcare Documentation Integrity
© 2010
Order: www.ahdionline.org

Human Diseases, 2nd Edition
Author: John H. Dirckx, MD
Publisher: Health Professions Institute
©2003
Order: www.hpisum.com

Laboratory Tests & Diagnostic Procedures in Medicine
Author: John H. Dirckx, MD
Publisher: Health Professions Institute
©2004
Order: www.hpisum.com

Medical Transcription Fundamentals: Where Success Takes Root, 2nd Edition
Author: Diane Gilmore
Publisher: Wolters Kluwer Health|Lippincott Williams & Wilkins
©2009
Order: www.stedmans.com

Principles of Anatomy & Physiology, 13th Edition
Authors: Gerard J. Tortora & Bryan Derrickson
Publisher: John Wiley & Sons, Inc.
©2009, 2012

Stedman's Medical Terminology: Steps to Success in Medical Language
Editor: Charlotte Creason, RHIA
Publisher: Wolters Kluwer Health|Lippincott Williams & Wilkins
©2011
Order: www.stedmans.com

Technology for the Medical Transcriptionist
Author: Laura Bryan, MT (ASCP), CMT, AHDI-F
Publisher: Wolters Kluwer Health|Lippincott Williams & Wilkins
©2010
Order: www.stedmans.com

The AMA Manual of Style: A Guide for Authors and Editors, 10th Edition
Author: Iverson, et al
Publisher: American Medical Association
©2007
Order: www.amamanualofstyle.com

The Book of Style for Medical Transcription, 3rd Edition
Author: Lea M. Sims, CMT, AHDI-F
Publisher: Association for Healthcare Documentation Integrity
©2008
Order: www.ahdionline.org

The Book of Style 3rd Edition Workbook: Practical Application & Assessment
Author: Lea M. Sims, CMT, AHDI-F
Publisher: Association for Healthcare Documentation Integrity
©2010
Order: www.ahdionline.org

The Gregg Reference Manual, 11th Edition
Author: Bill Sabin
Publisher: McGraw-Hill
©2011
Order: www.mhhe.com/business/buscom/gregg

The Language of Medicine, 9th edition
Author: Davi-Ellen Chabner, BA, MAT
Publisher: Elsevier, Inc.
©2011
Order: www.us.elsevierhealth.com

The Medical Transcription Workbook, 3rd Edition
Publisher: Health Professions Institute
©2010
Order: www.hpisum.com

Understanding Pharmacology for Health Professions, 3rd Edition
Author: Susan M. Turley
Publisher: Prentice Hall
©2002
Order: www.prenhall.com

Appendix B – Credentialing Overview

AHDI offers two voluntary credentials for medical transcription practitioners:

- Registered Medical Transcriptionist (RMT) – Level 1
- Certified Medical Transcriptionist (CMT) – Level 2

AHDI offers voluntary credentialing exams to individuals who wish to demonstrate job readiness and level-specific competency to prospective employers, clients, and industry colleagues. In offering credentialing exams for medical transcriptionists, AHDI is protecting the public interest by promoting professional standards, improving the practice of medical transcription, and recognizing those professionals who demonstrate competency through the fulfillment of stated requirements.

AHDI exams are delivered by Kryterion, a full-service test development and delivery company that provides world-class online testing technology integrating item banking, test delivery, and real-time reports; while leveraging a global network of testing centers. Kryterion is the market leader in live Online Proctoring (OLP), which utilizes remote video monitoring to observe test takers where they live, learn, or work.

The credentialing department at AHDI determines individual eligibility for exam admission. Based on test specifications developed by AHDI, Kryterion prepares and administers the individual tests approved by AHDI. Kryterion is also responsible for procuring and maintaining testing sites and overseeing online proctoring, test security, test administration, and related functions.

Visit the AHDI website at www.ahdionline.org and click on "Certification" for complete exam information and pricing. Interested persons should download and review the complete Credentialing Candidate Guide before scheduling your exam.

Appendix C - RMT Exam Blue Print Checklist

RMT candidates preparing for access to the RMT exam should adopt a study approach that incorporates preparation against the exam blue print. All questions a candidate will encounter on the RMT exam were strictly written against this blue print. Use the following checklist to assist you as you study each competency domain, marking the check box for each objective when you feel you have mastered the objective and have a strong working knowledge of concepts and information that fall within that domain area.

Section 1	Transcription Standards and Style	Studied Content Resources?	Completed Assessments?
1.1	Given sample report content or a subheading, identify the report type (*autopsy, consultation, correspondence, discharge summary, history and physical examination, operative report, pathology report, or SOAP note*) that the information would be transcribed under.		
1.2	Given sample report content, identify the correctly expressed report headings or subheadings.		
1.3	Identify the role/purpose of time and date stamping in transcription.		
1.4	Given dictated sentences, identify the one that would require editing on the part of the transcriptionist.		
1.5	Given dictated sentences, identify the one that contains an incorrectly used term, transposed terms or values, slang term or back formation.		
1.6	Given an audio excerpt containing a slang term, back formation, incorrectly used term, or transposed terms or values, fill in the blank(s) representing omitted information.		
1.7	Given a scenario of encountering a contextual inconsistency or irreconcilable word or phrase, identify the proper procedure for correction and/or notification.		
1.8	Given abbreviations related to health record privacy, identify the correct expanded form.		
1.9	Identify appropriate examples of PHI and/or disclosure of PHI under the HIPAA privacy rule.		
1.10	Identify the individuals and/or organizations that are defined as accountable parties or business associates under the HIPAA rule.		
1.11	Identify appropriate security measures for protecting PHI.		

1.12	Identify the recommended encryption standard of healthcare records under the HIPAA security rule.		
1.13	Identify documentation authentication practices considered dangerous by both the Joint Commission and DHHS.		
1.14	Given sentences with usage errors (subject/verb agreement, pronoun/antecedent agreement, who vs. whom, etc), identify the one containing correct usage.		
1.15	Given sentences containing English words commonly confused for other words, identify the correct sentence.		
1.16	Given an audio excerpt containing an incorrectly used English term, fill in the blank(s) representing omitted information.		
1.17	Given sentences or phrases, select the one that represents correct use of punctuation.		
1.18	Given words or sentences, identify the one that represents correct expression of capitalization.		
1.19	Given words or sentences, identify the one that reflects correct expression of a plural; or given a Latin singular form, identify the correct plural form; or given a Latin plural form, identify the correct singular form.		
1.20	Given words or sentences, identify the one that reflects correct expression of a possessive.		
1.21	Given an audio excerpt containing an incorrect singular or plural form, fill in the blank(s) representing omitted information.		
1.22	Given a definition, identify the correct Latin abbreviation, or given a Latin abbreviation, identify the correct definition.		
1.23	Given sentences containing dictated abbreviations, identify the one that requires expansion under the DIAGNOSIS or OPERATIVE TITLE headings.		
1.24	Identify the abbreviations found on the Joint Commission's *Do Not Use* list of dangerous abbreviations.		
1.25	Given an audio excerpt containing an incorrectly used abbreviation, fill in the blank(s) representing omitted information.		
1.26	Given numeric values or sentences containing numeric values, identify the one that reflects correct expression of a number or numbers.		

1.27	Given a sentence where the numeric value is a blank, identify the correct numeric expression to fill in the blank, or given a dictated word, phrase, or sentence containing a numeric value, identify the correctly transcribed expression of a numeric value.		
1.28	Given military time, identify the equivalent standard time, or given a standard time, identify the equivalent military time.		
1.29	Given numeric expressions, identify whether a roman numeral or an arabic numeral is required.		
1.30	Given an audio excerpt containing a numeric value, fill in the blank(s) representing omitted information.		
1.31	Given sentences, identify the one containing the correct expression of a percent, proportion, ratio, or numeric range, or given a dictated excerpt containing an underlined proportion or range, identify the correctly transcribed expression.		
1.32	Given an audio excerpt containing a percent, proportion, ratio, or range, fill in the blank(s) representing omitted information.		
1.33	Given a metric unit, identify the property it measures; or given a property, identify the metric unit by which it is measured; or given sentences, identify the one that represents correct expression of a metric or standard unit of measure.		
1.34	Given a sentence where the numeric value is blank, identify the correct expression of the numeric value and unit of measure.		
1.35	Given an audio excerpt containing a unit of measure, fill in the blank(s) representing omitted information.		
Section 2	**Clinical Medicine**	**Studied Content Resources?**	**Completed Assessments?**
2.1	Given the meaning of a word, identify the correct prefix, suffix, combining word, or root word, or given a prefix, suffix or combining form, and a definition, identify what is needed to create another given word.		
2.2	Given a medical term, identify the definition, or given a definition, identify the correct medical term.		
2.3	Given sentences, identify the correct use of a medical term commonly confused for another.		

2.4	Given a directional term, an anatomical position term, or a body plane term, identify the correct definition, or given a definition, identify the correct directional term, the correct anatomical position term, or the correct body plane term.		
2.5	Given an audio excerpt containing a clinical term, fill in the blank(s) representing omitted information.		
2.6	Given a laboratory panel, identify the tests associated with that panel or identify the tests that are part of a laboratory panel.		
2.7	Given a laboratory test, identify the normal values, or given a laboratory result, identify if the value is low, high, or normal.		
2.8	Given an audio excerpt containing a laboratory term, fill in the blank(s) representing omitted information.		
2.9	Given an imaging study type, identify the use or definition of that study type.		
2.10	Given an imaging study, identify common abbreviations and terminology associated with that study.		
2.11	Given an audio excerpt containing an imaging term, fill in the blank(s) representing omitted information.		
2.12	Given a drug or drug type, identify the route or form of administration, or given a route or form of administration, identify the drug or drug type.		
2.13	Given a drug term, identify the definition, or given a definition of a drug term, identify the term.		
2.14	Given a drug's generic name, identify the brand name, or given a drug's brand name, identify the generic name.		
2.15	Given a drug, identify the pharmacological category.		
2.16	Given an audio excerpt containing a pharmacology term, fill in the blank(s) representing omitted information.		
2.17	Given a clinical term, identify the correct definition, or given a definition, identify the correct clinical term. *See medical specialties above.*		
2.18	Given a clinical abbreviation, identify the correct term, or given a term, identify the correct clinical abbreviation. *See medical specialties above.*		
2.19	Given an audio excerpt containing any clinical term or abbreviation from a medical specialty, fill in the blank(s) representing omitted information. *See medical specialties above.*		

2.20	Given a graphic showing anatomy or systems, identify the anatomy or system involved.		
2.21	Given a position or location, identify the anatomical part of the human body.		
2.22	Given a physiologic process, identify steps or functions related to that process.		
2.23	Given a sign or symptom, identify the disease or syndrome.		
2.24	Given a disease or syndrome, identify the treatment course.		
2.25	Given a diagnostic test including laboratory studies, identify what is being measured.		
2.26	Given an audio excerpt containing a diagnostic test, fill in the blank(s) representing omitted information.		
2.27	Given a medication, identify the symptom or disease for which it is prescribed, or given a symptom or disease, identify the medication that is prescribed.		
2.28	Given a classification system, identify the expressed score or grade, or given a classification system result, identify the disease or affected anatomical part.		
2.29	Given an audio excerpt containing a classification system or treatment term, fill in the blank(s) representing omitted information.		
Section 3	**Health Information Technology**	**Studied Content Resources?**	**Completed Assessments?**
3.1	Given the abbreviation of a computer term, identify the correct expanded form.		
3.2	Given a computer technology term, identify the correct definition, or given a definition, identify the correct computer technology term.		
3.3	Given the abbreviation of a healthcare documentation technology term, identify the correct expanded form.		
3.4	Given a healthcare documentation technology term, identify the correct definition, or given a definition, identify the correct healthcare documentation technology term.		
3.5	Given a term or abbreviation related to transcription technology or data exchange, identify the correct definition, or given a definition related to transcription technology or data exchange, identify the term or abbreviation.		

Appendix D – AHDI's Statement on Verbatim Transcription

AHDI's Position

AHDI opposes the growing trend among healthcare facilities toward adopting a "verbatim" transcription policy, one that limits medical transcriptionists (MTs) to transcribing exactly what is dictated, regardless of error, and flagging all discrepancies for review by the dictator. AHDI believes this restricted role for documentation specialists ignores the contribution to risk management that MTs are trained and equipped to provide. A skilled, engaged MT partners with the dictating provider to ensure an accurate, timely, and secure record. Healthcare providers and facilities would be well served to recognize this contribution and empower MTs to be actively engaged in the story-telling of the patient encounter, noting discrepancies in grammar, style, and clinical information, and correcting those discrepancies that fall within the scope of the MT's knowledge and informed judgment.

Rationale

Routing discrepancies back to the dictator that could have been reasonably corrected by the transcriptionist has a direct impact on turn-around time and reimbursement. A significant delay in document work flow from patient encounter to reimbursement results when any record is flagged for provider review and correction. In an environment where even minor discrepancies must be flagged for review, the impact on turn-around time leads to backlog and delayed billing. Such a restrictive policy for editing and correction can be costly to the facility and burdensome to the medical records department that has to facilitate those corrections. MTs are risk management professionals equipped with an interpretive medical language skill set that should be *deployed*, not restricted, in the medical records setting to (a) ensure the accurate capture of clinical data, and (b) facilitate the forward progress of the record through the system.

Guidelines for MT Editing

AHDI recognizes that MTs are *not* engaged in provision of patient care and cannot be expected to have insight into the patient encounter beyond what is provided by the dictator. However, many discrepancies encountered in dictation represent areas of obvious error where correction falls within the scope of the interpretive skill set and clinical knowledge of the MT.

The Book of Style for Medical Transcription, 3rd Edition, provides the following editing guidelines to MTs when addressing discrepancies in dictation:

Editing	Verbatim transcription of dictation is seldom possible. MTs should prepare reports that are as correct, clear, consistent, and complete as can be reasonably expected, without imposing their personal style on those reports. Editing is inappropriate in medical transcription when it alters information without the editor's being certain of the appropriateness or accuracy of the change, when it second-guesses the originator, when it deletes appropriate and/or essential information, and when it tampers with the originator's style. Edit grammar, punctuation, spelling, and similar dictation errors as necessary to achieve clear communication. Likewise, edit slang words and phrases, incorrect terms, incomplete phrases, English or medical inconsistencies, and inaccurate phrasing of laboratory data.
Dictation Problems	A variety of dictation problems may occur, and a medical transcriptionist being alert to them is a form of risk management. Watch for and correct obvious errors in dictation, including grammar, spelling, terminology, and style. When uncertain, draw suspected errors to the attention of the originator and/or supervisor. When the change would be significant, particularly if it would influence medical meaning, leave a blank and flag it. Never "close up" the space where the unintelligible word, phrase, or sentence belongs, making it appear that a transcript is complete. Likewise, do not transcribe the questionable dictation, adding [sic] to indicate it is transcribed verbatim. When the transcriptionist cannot determine how to edit the incorrect dictation properly, sometimes the best choice is to leave a blank and flag it. Appropriate use of blanks should prompt careful followup and contribute to patient care and risk management. A medical transcriptionist who identifies an inconsistency in dictation should resolve it if this can be done with competence and

	confidence. If the discrepancy cannot be resolved with certainty, the report should be flagged and brought to the attention of the supervisor or the report's originator for resolution.

Honoring a physician's dictation style, recognizing error or inconsistency in the record, correcting errors appropriately, refraining from correcting or altering what cannot be confirmed, protecting the integrity of the patient encounter, and ensuring the confidentiality of the record define what a skilled, qualified medical transcriptionist is engaged in every day. AHDI encourages facilities who currently embrace verbatim transcription to replace this policy with one that provides clear guidelines for appropriate editing that empowers their MTs to be a contributory part of the risk management process.

Appendix E – AHDI Membership

The Association for Healthcare Documentation Integrity (AHDI) is a not-for-profit professional association incorporated in California in February 1978, with headquarters in Modesto, California. AHDI offers information about the profession of medical transcription, provides continuing education for medical transcriptionists, and enhances communication among those allied with the profession of medical transcription.

There are a number of resources available to the healthcare documentation expert in today's Internet age. More than ever before, an MT has access to new terminology, advances in clinical medicine, and changes and trends in the industry through online networking. But these resources cannot fully inform or prepare the conscientious practitioner for trends, drivers, and changes in any industry. Navigating the sea of information related to technology, standards, professional development, etc., can be difficult to manage alone. Associations exist to provide practitioners of a given industry the opportunity to work in concert toward the same goals.

AHDI offers its practitioners the opportunity for and access to resources, information, events, and services that empower them to make informed choices that lead to successful career outcomes. Together, we work to advance the profession through legislative advocacy, standard-setting, and professional development. While AHDI members receive many tangible benefits (publications, discounts, etc.), the decision to become a member of any professional association should be based on more than a desire for tangible benefits. The decision to commit your personal resources toward AHDI membership should reflect the following:

- Support of the mission, goals and objectives of the organization
- Desire to become part of a proactive body of practitioners working toward advancing the profession and driving change in the industry
- Need for information, services, products, and programs that will empower you as a practitioner
- Need for networking and personnel connection with your industry peers, particularly if you are an at-home, isolated practitioner

Find out more about AHDI and sign up online today by visiting our website – www.ahdionline.org or calling our toll free number 800-982-2182.

Appendix F – AHDI Product Highlights

The Book of Style for Medical Transcription, 3rd edition

$50.00 members
$70.00 nonmembers

The 3rd edition of The Book of Style for Medical Transcription from the Association for Healthcare Documentation Integrity (AHDI) is now available in print and in a web-based electronic version. This widely acclaimed industry standards manual has long been the trusted resource for data capture and documentation standards in healthcare. The 3rd edition delivers a streamlined and strategically reorganized flow of critical data, enhanced explanation of standards and practical application, robust examples taken from clinical medicine settings, and so much more.

The Book of Style Workbook

$35.00 members
$50.00 nonmembers

This companion workbook to *The Book of Style for Medical Transcription, 3rd edition*, is designed to work in tandem with the Book of Style. The *Workbook* contains practical application exercises to assist students, postgraduates, and working MTs with orientation to standards and preparation for AHDI credentialing exams.

Mega MT Challenge I & II

$35.00 members, $45.00 nonmembers (Each individual CD)
$60.00 members, $80.00 nonmembers (Combo Deal)

These electronic CDs contain over 1200 questions (combined) related to the practice of medical transcription. You'll find questions pertaining to medical terminology, English fundamentals, pharmacology, and an array of medical specialties. A broad variety of question formats (including multiple-choice, true/false, circle one, fill in the blank, etc.) are designed to fully test the wealth of knowledge essential to the practice of transcription. Whether used for self-study, exam preparation, evaluation, staff training, potential employee testing, or classroom instruction, these products are designed to help meet those needs. Order online or by phone.

CMT Prep Quizzes, Volume I, II, III

$25.00 members (each CD)
$35.00 nonmembers (each CD)
Bundle Pricing Available Online

Each CD contains a whopping 240 exam-style questions, answers, and descriptions as found in archived publications. This interactive CD allows you to take the quiz on screen, view the answers and descriptions Makes for great level II prep questions, as well as practice with on-screen test taking. Order online or by phone.

Willie Getwell

$25.00 members
$35.00 nonmembers

This CD provides proofreading and editing exercises designed to enhance your skill in the area of editing and error recognition. You will find 40 transcribed and speech-recognized drafts to orient you to the unique editing and proofing process associated with both domains. Product is perfect for getting your editing up to speed before testing. Order online or by phone.

CMT Prep Assessment Online Course

$100.00 members
$125.00 nonmembers

Offered every month of the year, this four-week course is designed to assist individuals preparing for the CMT exam. Course offers assessment in over 20 body systems. Each body system covered will list websites, medical texts, and references from *The Book of Style for Medical Transcription, 3e,* where applicable. Register online or by phone.

RMT Prep Assessment Online Course

$75.00 members
$100.00 nonmembers

Offered every month of the year, this four-week course is designed to assist individuals preparing for the RMT exam and offers assessment in the areas covered in the RMT exam blueprint. Register online or by phone.

Medicolegal Flashcards
$25.00 members
$35.00 nonmembers

AHDI ***Flash Cards*** are designed to provide the student, new graduate, and/or seasoned MT with quick, high-impact study tools for skill-building and exam preparation. Take this handy, convenient pack of easy-to-use flash cards with you when you travel, have a long wait in a doctor's office or kids' soccer practice, or just need to make the most of that 10 minutes between appointments. Each set of flashcards covers a content area on the AHDI exam blueprint and is designed to put that core knowledge right at your fingertips. This set of medicolegal flash cards will test your knowledge and understanding of a broad range of medicolegal concepts and terms associated with the healthcare delivery and the documentation sector including such topics as: ***HIPAA, document types, document formats, the legal record, malpractice, DNRs***, and many more.

To find out more or order any product above, visit www.ahdionline.org. You can also call AHDI at 1-800-982-2182 to place an order by phone.

CPSIA information can be obtained
at www.ICGtesting.com
Printed in the USA
FSHW022342031020
74364FS